INDIAN CASTE CUSTOMS

Owing to the antiquity and rarity of this book, certain pages are regrettably absent, and readability is compromised due to the blurring of the original text. If you possess any insights regarding the availability of these missing sections, kindly inform us. Your assistance is crucial in ensuring the completion of this significant work for the benefit of future generations.

INDIAN CASTE CUSTOMS

L. S. S. O'MALLEY

GYAN

Published by

Gyan Publishing House
5, Ansari Road
Daryaganj, New Delhi-110002
Phone: 011-47034999, 9811692060
E-mail: books@gyanbooks.com

Distribution Network
gyanbooks.com
India, USA, Canada, UK, Australia

ISBN: 978-93-6780-970-9 (HB)

First Published, 1932

2nd Impression 2024

Printed at: Gyan Press, Delhi.

INDIAN CASTE CUSTOMS
Author: L. S. S. O'MALLEY

INDIAN CASTE CUSTOMS

INDIAN CASTE CUSTOMS

By

L. S. S. O'MALLEY
C.I.E., I.C.S. *retired*

CAMBRIDGE
AT THE UNIVERSITY PRESS
1932

CONTENTS

PREFACE

THERE is an extraordinary difference of opinion as to the merits and demerits of the Indian caste system. On the one hand, a man as careful in his judgments as Sir Henry Maine condemned the system in *Ancient Law* as "the most disastrous and blighting of all human institutions". Rabindra Nath Tagore has described it as "a gigantic system of cold-blooded repression", and is of opinion that the regeneration of the Indian people, directly and perhaps solely, depends upon its removal. In *Problems of British India* M. Joseph Chailley expressed the view that caste bars out altruism, unity and patriotism, and that its rules render true social life and progress impossible. On the other hand, Sir Monier Monier-Williams observed in *Brahmanism and Hinduism* that "caste has been useful in promoting self-sacrifice, in securing subordination of the individual to an organized body, in restraining from vice, in preventing pauperism". Meredith Townsend wrote in *Europe and Asia*: "I firmly believe caste to be a marvellous discovery, a form of socialism which through ages has protected Hindoo society from anarchy and from the worst evils of industrial and competitive life—it is an automatic poor-law to begin with and the strongest form known of trades union".

It is difficult to obtain a complete conspectus of actual caste regulations and practices which might explain the reasons for such differences of opinion. Ethnological works on the subject of caste are apt to deal less with points of detail than with more general matters such as the different types of castes and questions of origin. Valuable information is contained in M. Emile Senart's brilliant monograph, *Caste in India*, and in the Indian Census Reports, especially those of 1911, which embodied the results of special inquiries into caste government; but the former is brief—its author modestly calls it "merely a sketch"—the latter are many in number and not readily accessible to the general reader. Few persons perhaps outside India have an extensive knowledge of the way in which the caste system operates in every-day life, e.g., what are its injunctions and prohibitions, what actions constitute offences against its code of moral law and social honour, what are the means by which breaches of that code are adjudicated, and what are the penalties inflicted on offenders. In the following pages, in writing which, as I desire to acknowledge most fully, I have been very largely indebted to the Indian Census Reports and District Gazetteers, I have endeavoured to give some account of the working of the caste system in the hope of adding to the ordinary man's knowledge of this peculiar form of social organization and of enabling him to form a judgment of its merits and defects.

L. S. S. O'MALLEY

Chapter I

THE CASTE SYSTEM

THE word "caste" is of Portuguese origin, being a form of *casta*, meaning race or breed, a word which the early Portuguese settlers in India used to describe the different sections of the Hindu community. A decree issued by the Sacred Council of Goa in 1567 stated that in some parts of the province of Goa the Hindus were divided into distinct *castas* of greater or less dignity, which were maintained so superstitiously that no one of a higher could eat or drink with those of a lower; and Garcia de Orta wrote in 1563 that no one changed from his father's trade and that all those of the same *casta* of shoemakers were the same.[1]

These references to the caste system bring out some of its salient features, viz. that Hindu society is divided into a number of distinct sections known as castes, which are regarded as high and low according to their position in the social scale, and that members of the same caste eat and drink together but not with members of an inferior caste. Another fact to which they

1 Loc. cit. H. Yule and A. C. Burnell, *Hobson-Jobson* (1903), p. 171.

draw attention is of more particular and less general application, viz. that some castes have a common hereditary occupation or handicraft. Curiously enough, however, the most important and distinctive feature of the caste system is not mentioned, viz. that of marriage within the caste, the rule of endogamy, according to which men must marry women of their own caste and of no other. This is an almost invariable rule, but there are exceptions, for some castes, consisting of aborigines who have been Hinduized, practice exogamy, i.e. a man must marry a woman of another caste. It is exclusiveness as regards both marriage and social intercourse which makes caste such a peculiar form of social organization, one to which there is no parallel in the modern world.

Not only is caste the basis of Hindu society, but it has affected the Indian Moslem social organization. The idea of caste is alien to Islam, which rests on the principle of religious equality and brotherhood; but in spite of this there are some groups among the Moslems which observe caste restrictions on intermarriage to such an extent that a man of a higher group may be degraded to a lower group if he takes a wife from it; in some parts also members of one group will not eat with another. These groups, however, cannot be regarded as true castes, although they have some of the characteristics of the caste system.

At the census of 1901 it was found that there were altogether 2378 tribes and castes in India, some with numbers running into millions and others of microscopic size. There are over fourteen million Brahmans alone. The next most numerous caste is that of the Chamars (eleven millions), who work in hides and leather and are at the bottom of the social scale. The third is that of the Rajputs (nearly ten millions), who rank next to the Brahmans. After the census of 1901 the practice of tabulating figures for every tribe and caste, however small, was abandoned, as it was thought that to do so for small or even minute communities, representing a negligible or infinitesimal proportion of the population, involved an expenditure of time, labour and money which was not justified by the practical value of the results obtained. Separate statistics are now compiled only for tribes and castes reaching a certain figure or representing a certain percentage of the total population.

Whatever the aggregate of castes may be, it does not exhaust the number of mutually exclusive social groups among the Hindus. So far from being a homogeneous whole, a caste is generally subdivided into sections called subcastes, most of which are replicas of the main caste both in the matter of food and drink and nearly all in the more important matter of intermarriage, for the members of each sub-caste marry only fellow-members of the sub-caste. There are some exceptions to this general rule. Some castes of a tribal type, such as the Rajputs, have subdivisions which practise exogamy, men obtaining their wives from other sections of the caste. Certain castes of aboriginal origin, the descendants of aboriginal tribes which have been Hinduized, are also subdivided into exogamous sects of a totemistic type. In other words, the septs bear the names of animals, birds, trees, plants and various objects, the killing, cutting or use of which is taboo; and the men of one sept may only marry a woman of another sept with a different totem. A typical example of such totemism is furnished by the Bagdis in the west of Bengal, who have exogamous septs bearing the names of the heron, jungle-cock, bean, tortoise and a certain kind of fish. One sept may not kill or eat a heron, another may not eat beans, etc. Another caste, the Bauris, found in the same tract of country, reveres both the heron and the dog. Killing a heron involves expulsion from the caste, and a Bauri will neither kill a dog not touch its dead body. Should a dog be accidentally drowned in a reservoir, its water cannot be used until it has been purified by months of monsoon rain.

A sub-caste is very much less important than a caste. A man's caste determines his place in Hindu society, and consequently his relations with all other Hindus. His sub-caste affects only his relations with fellow-members of his caste. No one indeed troubles about a man's sub-caste except members of his own caste. The dividing lines between sub-castes are also less sharply defined than those between castes; their rules and customs are far more subject to change. Some sub-castes, for example, will eat and drink together; others will relax the rule of endogamy and allow intermarriage if, for example, there is a shortage of marriageable girls in a particular sub-caste. When, as is usually the case, the rule of endogamy is maintained, the punishment for marrying outside the sub-caste is less severe than for marrying outside the caste. The laws of a caste on the subject of intermarriage are like those of the Medes and Persians, but those of the sub-caste vary not only from time to time but also from place to place, e.g. a sub-caste may be endogamous in one part of the country and exogamous in another. At present castes among whose members education has spread are tending to withdraw the ban on marriages between members of different sub-castes as a measure of reform.

The sub-castes themselves are subdivided into various exogamous groups, often of large numbers; there are, for example, one hundred and twenty exogamous divisions in one sub-caste of the Gauras, a cowherd caste in Orissa.

Two kinds of exogamy are general—*gotra* exogamy and *sapinda* exogamy. Under the rule of *gotra* exogamy, which is in force among Brahmans and other castes observing Brahmanical marriage customs, there can be no marriage within the *gotra* (also called *got*, *mul* and *kul*), which consists of those who have, or who are believed to have, a common ancestor, generally mythical, whose name the *gotra* usually bears. A man must therefore marry a woman who belongs to his sub-caste but not to his *gotra*; marriage to any one of the same *gotra* is regarded almost in the light of incest. *Sapinda* exogamy prohibits marriage of kindred or affinity within a certain number of generations both on the father's side and on the mother's side. A standard formula in North India among castes of good standing is that there must be no marriage either within seven degrees on the father's side or within five degrees on the mother's side, but some authorities allow the latter number to be reduced to three. Even so the list of prohibited degrees is much longer than that prescribed by the Christian churches and by Islam.[1]

There is not the same straitness of rule and practice in South India, where many castes recognize what are called cross cousin marriages. This means that a man may, and in some cases

[1] For a full treatment of the subject see S. V. Karandikar, *Hindu Exogamy* (Bombay, 1928).

must, marry the daughter of either his maternal uncle or his paternal aunt, while his sister marries the son of her maternal uncle or paternal aunt. With a few exceptions cross cousin marriage is restricted to these relationships, and marriages between the children of two brothers or between the children of two sisters are prohibited.[1] The custom helps to keep property in the family and to keep down the expenses incidental to a marriage, such as the payment of a price for a bride or bridegroom and lavish entertainment, and on account of these advantages it is said to have found its way even into Brahman circles.[2] Some castes, such as the Kammavans, go further and hold that a man should marry either one of the two cousins above mentioned or his sister's daughter. A Kammavan boy is sometimes married to a woman old enough to be his mother. His father then begets children for him, but the boy is regarded as their legal father. Another curious feature of this system is that if there is an excess of women in a family, a man may have to marry several wives in order to

[1] Inquiries made in the south of the Bombay Presidency in 1911 showed that thirty-one castes allowed a man to marry the daughter of a maternal uncle or paternal aunt, that three also allowed marriage to the daughter of a maternal aunt, and that fifteen allowed a man to marry the daughter of a maternal uncle but no other cousin.

[2] Rao Bahadur Anantha Krishna Iyer, *Lectures on Ethnography* (Calcutta, 1925), p. 130.

remove the disgrace which attaches to a family if its women remain unmarried.[1]

Some high castes are distinguished by what is called hypergamy. This is a term coined by Mr Coldstream and first used by Sir Denzil Ibbetson in his *Report on the Census of the Punjab in 1881*, in which he defined it as the law of superior marriage. It is now more generally described as "marrying up", and it means the unwritten law by which a woman must be married to a man belonging to a group superior, or at least equal, to her own. Hypergamy is, therefore, a more comprehensive term than would appear from its derivation, for it covers the marriage of a girl to a man in the same class as well as marriage to one in a higher class. The essential thing is that a woman must not have her status lowered by marrying into a group of lower rank. Parents who fail to observe this rule are liable to be reduced to the group into which their daughters marry.

The effect of the rule is that the women of the highest of a number of groups have a narrower circle within which to marry than the women of lower groups, who can marry men of any of the groups above them as well as of their own group. In the highest groups, therefore, there are apt to be a surplus of marriageable girls and a deficiency of eligible bridegrooms. The law of supply

[1] *District Gazetteer of Tinnevelly* (1917), p. 143.

and demand comes into operation, with the result that the value of husbands is enhanced and marriage becomes a matter of competitive price. Bridegrooms have to be paid for by the fathers of brides, whereas among the low castes, which have no custom of hypergamy, a "bride price" is usually paid by the bridegroom's parents. Both among the high and the low castes there is a marriage market, as bridegrooms among the former and brides among the latter command prices which vary according to their social position, affluence and attainments.

Hypergamy has been a source of grave abuses. It is a solemn duty, enjoined by his religion, for a Hindu father to have his daughters married. The fulfilment of this duty is complicated by the law of hypergamy, which in the higher groups of a caste limits the choice of possible husbands and also increases the expense of obtaining them. The Rajputs of Rajputana and elsewhere, faced with the difficulty of getting their daughters married, either because of a shortage of unmarried males in the higher groups or because of their own lack of means, used to practise female infanticide. The Kulin branch of Brahmans in Bengal found a more humane solution of the problem in polygamy. It was the custom for Kulin men to have a plurality of wives, who were maintained by their fathers and visited occasionally by their husbands. Vidyasagar, a social reformer of the early part of the nineteenth century, who laboured to put an end to the practice, mentioned the case of five men in one village who between them had altogether 230 wives. A Kulin Brahman who had an embarrassing number of female relatives is known to have had eighteen of them (six aunts, eight sisters and four daughters) married in a batch to a boy ten years old—truly a case of mass marriage. Kulinism, as the practice is called, has nearly died out owing to the spread of education and enlightened ideas, and also, according to Jogendra Nath Bhattacharya, owing to material considerations. "The *coup de grâce*", he wrote in *Hindu Castes and Tribes* (1896), "has been given to the practice by a decision of the Bengal High Court declaring that according to the law of the Shastras[1] applicable to Hindus even the Kulins are bound to give maintenance to their wives." He also left it on record that there were still some Kulin Brahmans who had such large numbers of wives as to necessitate their keeping regular registers for refreshing their memories about the names and residences of their spouses. The practice, though now very rare, is not altogether extinct in Bengal. The writer was informed in 1911 by a Bengali gentleman that he knew personally three Kulin Brahmans, of whom one had

[1] Ancient Hindu law-books.

married sixty, the second eight, and the third four wives. It survives, however, among the Maithil Brahmans of North Bihar. Among them there is a class of men known as Bikauwas or venders because they sell themselves, or their sons, in marriage to girls of lower groups for an agreed price. Some make a living in this way and have been known to have forty or fifty wives, who live with their parents and are not supported by their husbands. The latter have to pocket their pride for the sake of the money they make, for they are not received on equal terms by fellow Brahmans and a family of which the men habitually marry girls of a lower group sinks to its level.

Next to the rules regarding intermarriage and commensality, perhaps the most distinctive feature of the caste system is the way in which different castes are ranked in an order of social dignity. There is a graduated scale culminating in the Brahman and descending to what are known as the untouchables or depressed classes. There is no detailed warrant of precedence in which each individual caste has an assigned place, but rather a social stratification in which castes are grouped in different layers. The organization of Hindu society in different strata has ancient authority. The Laws of Manu (also called the Code of Manu or the Institutes of Manu), which Hindus believe to be of a divine revelation and revere as the highest authority on their ancient customs, stated that there were four *varnas*, or orders, in the social system, viz. in order of precedence, (1) the Brahmans, the priestly and learned class; (2) the Kshattriyas, the military and governing class; (3) the Vaisyas, who were traders and agriculturists, and kept cattle, and (4) the Sudras, who were the servants and menials of the three higher orders and were also engaged in industrial work. The first three were distinguished as "twice-born", i.e. besides having the physical birth common to all human beings, they had a second spiritual birth through being initiated into the mysteries of religion and invested with the sacred thread: this is a kind of string made up of strands of thread, which is looped over and hangs from the left shoulder.[1] The ceremony of investiture takes place when a boy is old enough to understand his duties and responsibilities, and has been aptly compared to the rite of confirmation in the Christian Church. The Sudras were "once-born"; they had no right therefore to wear the sacred thread, and they were regarded as a servile class, whose duty it was to minister to the twice-born. The institution of the four orders was looked upon as divine and immut-

[1] According to the Laws of Manu, the sacred thread of a Brahman must be made of cotton, that of a Kshattriya of *san* (hemp or flax) thread, and that of a Vaisya of woollen thread.

able: a great gulf was fixed between each, which none might pass.

Outside the four orders, and outside the pale of Hinduism, was a miscellaneous mass of outcasts. The lowest of these were the Chandals, who were not allowed to live within the village, and were regarded as the scum of the earth, little better, indeed, than the animals which they kept; it was laid down that they should keep only dogs and donkeys, then, as now, looked on as vile and unclean animals. They were doomed to a miserable existence not only in this life but also hereafter, for the offerings which Hindus make to secure the salvation of the soul after death might not be offered by them.

It must not be assumed that the Laws of Manu described the working of an actual system, for research has shown that they were compiled by Brahmans, who drew an ideal picture of what they thought the social organism should be rather than a portraiture of what it actually was, and presented the ideal as the real. It would not be safe therefore to postulate that the different communities had no subdivisions or castes in the modern sense of the word. The Laws of Manu indeed mention about fifty castes (*jāti*) as well as the four *varnas*, and there can be little doubt that castes co-existed with the latter. A parallel to the *varnas* may be found in the former social organization of Japan, which recognized four classes, viz. (1) the court nobles, who claimed descent from deities or emperors; (2) the military class; (3) the Heimin or common people, who were divided into cultivators, artisans and traders; and (4) a pariah class, engaged in despised occupations such as leather-work, which lived in separate villages and could neither intermarry nor eat with the higher classes.

It is the common belief of Hindus that the *varnas* were actually castes, and this belief has a far-reaching influence. The *varnas* were of divine creation, and consequently the caste system is also believed to have divine sanction. Certain castes are moreover recognized as being representatives of the Kshattriyas, Vaisyas and Sudras, and are treated accordingly, with respect or the reverse. Some therefore have pride of place in the social system as being twice-born and having the right to wear the sacred thread; others are once-born with no such right. Many of the latter, it is true, claim a higher status and arrogate the sacred thread, but this pretension is, as a rule, scouted both by ancient tradition and current opinion.

Those lower castes which are held to be the modern representatives of the Sudras are not all on the same level, for some are regarded as clean and others as unclean. This refers to ceremonial and not to physical purity, and it means that the touch of some castes is believed to defile members of higher castes, while that of others does not. Pollution so caused can, and should, be removed by ceremonial purification, such as bathing. No one of a twice-born caste, again, may drink water which has been touched or brought by an unclean Sudra, unless it is water from the river Ganges, which is of such sanctity as to be an exception to this rule. Brahmans may minister to clean Sudras, but not to the unclean, and the relative position of the low castes may therefore be gauged by their ability to employ Brahmans, or rather on the willingness of Brahmans to serve them. Conversely, the status of different sections of Brahmans in the Punjab is said to depend on the status of the castes to which they minister.[1] In this respect a distinction should be drawn between Brahmans of good standing and those of low standing. Some Brahmans are employed by unclean castes, but they are a kind of hedge-priests, are regarded by other Brahmans as degraded on this account, and are not received in communion by them.

Many of the lowest castes, belonging to the classes known as the untouchables, can get no Brahman to act as their priest and have priests of their own caste. They are not admitted inside Hindu temples having Brahman priests and a

[1] *Punjab Census Report for 1911*, Part 1, p. 310.

Brahmanical liturgy, and their gods or godlings do not come within the Brahmanical pantheon. These godlings are commonly represented by stocks and stones, which are set up in the open under a tree or shed; and they are propitiated by sacrifices of pigs and cocks, abhorrent to Brahmanism. The first rise up the social ladder is gained when the services of a Brahman priest, however low, are secured, under whose ministrations the sacrifices of animals give place to offerings of milk and rice, while the godling becomes identified with some regular Hindu god and is enshrined in a temple. A curious example of the way in which Brahmans become associated with non-Brahmanical worship may be mentioned. In Bengal there is a godling called Dharmaraj, who is very possibly of respectable Buddhist descent but who is now worshipped in the shape of a stone and credited with powers of healing. His priests are commonly men of the scavenger castes, such as Hari and Dom. In one district some Brahmans suffering from diseases believed to be incurable turned in despair to Dharmaraj, vowed to make offerings if cured, and were miraculously cured. They had to redeem their vows but would not make their votive offerings through the established priest, who was an untouchable Hari. A way out of the impasse was found by installing a low Brahman who was ready to associate himself with the Hari in order to make a living. The two became partners, each having a *clientèle* of his own, but the Brahman was the predominant partner, for he forced the Hari to make his sacrifices of pigs and cocks in the jungle behind the building housing Dharmaraj. Finally the Hari family died out and the Brahman remained in sole possession.

The halo of sanctity attaches to a Brahman of good status irrespective of his means and personal character and is reflected by the honorific title of Maharaj, or prince, by which he is commonly addressed in North India: the designation of Devi or goddess is prefixed to the names of Brahman women. In spite of the veneration in which they are held, the Brahmans are not immune from depreciation at the hands of Hindus of lower caste, who, while not questioning their spiritual and caste supremacy, have many proverbs satirizing their weaknesses; other castes, be it added, are dealt with equally faithfully and impartially. Typical proverbs of this kind, which are current in South Bihar, are "Give a Brahman clarified butter and he wriggles with delight"—an allusion to his greed; "Brahmans, dogs and bards (Bhats) are always quarrelling among themselves"; "The son of a Brahman is a fool till he is 52 years old"; "You can influence a Kayasth by bribes, a Brahman by feeding him well, a Rajput by flattery, but the low castes only by thrashing".[1] With this last may be compared another popular proverb, "Rice and *pān* (*Piper betel*) must be watered and the low castes kicked," which is equally eloquent of the ignominious treatment thought to be suitable for the low castes.

The inequalities of the caste system and the basic fact that a man's place in the social sphere is unalterably fixed by the accident of birth are justified to the Hindus by their belief in metempsychosis or the transmigration of souls combined with the doctrine of *Karma*, which asserts that each rebirth is the direct result of a man's actions in a previous existence. This life is but one in many, an insignificant portion of the total span of existence. There is an endless series of rebirths, and as a man sows, so shall he reap. A man's caste consequently depends on his actions in a previous life; worth in one life determines birth in another. This explains the inequalities of caste, why one man is born to honour, another to dishonour. The belief is based on the idea of predestination, and it induces acquiescence in the rights and disabilities attaching to one's birth. The general idea is, in fact, that one can be but what one is born to be. It is enjoined in the Hindu scriptures that a man

[1] C. E. A. W. Oldham, "The Proverbs of the People in a district (Shahabad) of Northern India", *Folk-Lore*, December, 1930.

should do his duty in that state of life which his caste determines for him; and those who do so are buoyed up by the hope that they may at a future rebirth be members of a higher caste.

Caste is not merely a social institution but part of Hinduism, which on that account has been described as a socio-religious system, for it is partly a social organization based on caste and partly a religious belief, or congeries of beliefs. Caste is, in fact, the steel frame binding together the many beliefs massed together in Hinduism. So integral a part is it of Hinduism, that a Hindu without a caste is almost a contradiction in terms. An ascetic, it is true, may rise to such a height in spiritual life as to be above the trammels of caste, but a layman cannot. A man may entertain Hinduistic beliefs, but unless he belongs to a caste, he cannot be a member of Hindu society. As observed by Barth, a caste is the express badge of Hinduism. "The man who is a member of a caste is a Hindu; he who is not, is not a Hindu."[1] Even if Hinduism could be considered purely as a religion, caste would still be a most important feature of it, because practice means more than dogma, and practice is a question of the observance of caste customs and regulations as well as of religious ceremonies. A Hindu may be a monotheist or pantheist, or even an atheist, in belief, and it

[1] *The Religions of India* (1882), Preface, p. xvii.

makes no difference provided he observes the rules of conduct laid down by his caste. Hinduism is elastic as regards belief but rigid as regards practice. Even the most orthodox have a wide tolerance for different shades of thought, but they insist on strictness in practice and observance. A Hindu may think as he likes, but he must not disobey the cardinal caste tenets concerning his marriage and method of life.

It is generally recognized that each caste has an innate right to lay down its own canons of conduct provided that they are in conformity with the basic principles of Hinduism and do not affect the rights or infringe the prerogatives of other castes. If these conditions are observed, no other caste has any business to interfere. Each maintains its own customs and respects those of others. The general idea is "live and let live". It excites no surprise that what is forbidden to one caste may be permissible or even obligatory in another. Practices vary not only from caste to caste but also within the same caste according to locality. There is rarely a general rule to which there is not an exception, and to add to the almost bewildering variety, which makes it as difficult as it is unsafe to generalize, castes found in one part of the country may be unknown in another, and the same caste may have a different place in the social hierarchy in different areas.

Despite all its diversity, the main mould of

caste is the same. Throughout India caste remains the basis of social order, with its numerous divisions, each of which has a social value in relation only to other divisions, its theocratic doctrine of the sanctity of the Brahman and its belief that a man's place in life is preordained. The differences are of form and not of substance; there is a fundamental unity of system, and it may well be said of caste: *Plus ça change, plus c'est la même chose.*

The caste system is especially rigid in South India, where it even affects the lay-out of villages. The houses of the Brahmans are in one quarter, those of the Sudra castes in another, and among the latter any caste that is sufficiently numerous will have a separate block. Just outside the village are the houses of less reputable castes; and in the fields, still further removed from the village site, cluster the huts of degraded castes like the Paraiyan (more familiar to the British in the form of Pariah). The caste system in South India is also distinguished by a unique feature. Many of the castes are divided into two sections called the right-hand (*Balagai*) and the left-hand (*Yedagai*) castes. To the right-hand section belong various cultivating and trading castes and also (by a strange conjunction considering their respectability) one of the lowest, the Paraiyan. To the left-hand group belong artisan castes, such as workers in various metals, stone and leather. Brahmans and other castes stand aloof and belong to neither section. The origin of the division is lost in the obscurity of past ages, and the differences between the two are now chiefly manifested in disputes about questions of privilege in connexion with ceremonies and their paraphernalia, such as the right to ride on horseback, or carry flags, in processions and the number of pillars (e.g. eleven or twelve) supporting the *pandals* or booths erected for marriage feasts. Quarrels often arise over such matters as the procession of one party down streets inhabited by the other, and have led before now to bloody conflicts, which in dimensions have approached pitched battles.

South India is more bigoted and reactionary than North India; ceremonial observances and caste distinctions are more closely kept up—a man of lower caste is even expected to be uncovered down to the waist in the presence of a Nambudri Brahman of Malabar[1]—and the doctrine of untouchability is carried to lengths unknown in the north. On this account, if no other, Madras may be said to deserve the name of "the benighted Presidency" which is often applied to it. Orissa is another home of conservatism and orthodoxy, largely because it was long isolated from close contact with the outside world and modernizing influences; the railway was not ex-

[1] *District Gazetteer of Malabar* (1908), p. 105.

tended to it till less than half a century ago. The Brahmans punctiliously observe the laws of ceremonial purity, but on the other hand the caste system is more fluid than in Madras or Bengal. It is possible not only for outsiders to be admitted into certain low castes but also for men of low caste to rise to higher castes, and intermarriages take place between castes of equal standing and even between some castes of higher and lower rank.

The caste system is least rigid and precise on the northern confines of the Indian Empire, in Assam, the Punjab and North-West Frontier Province, Kashmir, Sind and Nepal. It is unknown in Burma and Baluchistan except among immigrants from other parts of India. The greater part of Assam was occupied from an early period by tribes of Mongoloid origin, and the number of Brahmans and other high castes who settled in it was small. The Brahmanical leaven has not been enough to leaven the mass of the people, so that the standard of ceremonial and caste customs is not high. Assam is remarkable for the extent to which different castes intermarry; in the State of Manipur local Brahmans marry Kshattriya women without losing caste, and the children are also Brahmans; if a Brahman woman marries beneath her, she merely sinks to the level of her husband.

Caste in the Punjab plays a less important

part in social life than in other parts of India and is relegated to a subordinate position in areas where tribal units predominate. "In rural areas of the western Punjab society is organized on a tribal basis and caste hardly exists."[1] Conditions are similar in the North-West Frontier Province. In Sind there is said to be very little religion that would be recognized as Hinduism in the rest of India.[2] The Brahmans, so far from being noted for learning and piety, are described as illiterate and depraved; and the Lohanas, mainly traders by profession, who form the principal caste, have been so much affected by the influence of Moslem tribes which have overrun and ruled the country that "they wear the beard of the Muhammadan conqueror and permit themselves the luxury of animal food provided it has been slain after the orthodox fashion of Islam".[3] The Hindus of Kashmir are extraordinarily lax in many ways, and, as Sir Walter Lawrence has observed, do in their own country many things which would horrify an orthodox Hindu. Brahmans even drink water brought by Moslems, eat food cooked on a Moslem boat, employ Moslem foster nurses for their children,

[1] *Imperial Gazetteer*, vol. xx, p. 287.

[2] E. H. Aitken, *Gazetteer of the Province of Sind* (1907), p. 164.

[3] *Imperial Gazetteer*, vol. xxii, pp. 406, 407. Moslems eat the meat of animals which have been killed with a prayer uttered at the time of cutting the throat.

and in the villages do not scruple to drive the plough or carry manure.[1]

In Nepal, though it is Hindu in government and caste is the basis of social life, the people generally are not bound by its ties like the Hindus in other parts of India, but have liberal ideas and elastic practices in the matter of occupations, food and ceremonial rites. The upper classes are more orthodox. Their whole life is said to be ordered by caste, and "the decision to do such and such a thing, or to make such and such a journey, is based entirely on the effect such action will have upon caste".[2] The three higher castes, Brahmans, Chetris and Thakurs, set the standard for others, and the customs of the lower castes are becoming assimilated to theirs. The process has not gone very far; even the Chetris will not allow caste considerations to interfere with their military duties. What this means may be realized from a remark of Brian Houghton Hodgson, who was long resident in Nepal.

> These highland soldiers, who despatch their meal in half an hour, and satisfy the ceremonial law by merely washing their hands and face, and taking off their turbans before cooking, laugh at the pharisaical rigour of our *sipāhis*, who must bathe from head to foot and

[1] *The Valley of Kashmir* (1895), pp. 300, 303.

[2] W. Brook Northey and C. J. Morris, *The Gurkhas* (1928), p. 133.

make *pūja* ere they can begin to dress their dinner, must eat nearly naked in the coldest weather, and cannot be in marching trim again in less than three hours.[1]

Nepal is however a land of contrasts, for in other respects, notably in regard to marriage, the observance of Hindu customs is enforced by the State. Nepal is the only independent Hindu kingdom left in the world and its Government does not forget it, but takes a pride in maintaining the ordinances of early Hinduism. Its penal code is based on the *Sāstras* or ancient law-books, and its courts of justice punish transgressions of a social or religious character, as if they were criminal offences. Crimes are divided into three classes according as they affect the State, private persons or property, and caste. The killing of cows is punishable by death; Brahmans are immune from capital punishment, the severest penalty to which they are liable, even for murder, being imprisonment for life together with degradation from caste. The Judge of the Chief Court remarked to Hodgson:

> Below (i.e. in the plains of India) let any man and woman commit what sin they will, there is no punishment provided, no expiatory right enjoined. Hence Hinduism is destroyed; the distinctions of caste are

[1] The sepoys here referred to were high caste Hindus such as Brahmans and Rajputs. *Pūja* means the performance of ceremonies. *Essays on the Languages, Literature and Religion of Nepal and Tibet* (1874), p. 40.

obliterated. Here, on the contrary, all those distinctions are religiously preserved by the public courts of justice, which punish according to caste and never destroy the life of a Brahman. Below, the Shastras are things to talk of: here they are acted up to.[1]

There has been little change during the last century. Mr Perceval Landon writes in *Nepal* (1928):

In Nepal, where the tradition of life and thoughts is less changed from that of early India than elsewhere, the religious law still remains to permeate, and indeed to form the foundation of, the existing system of administration. However gross or infamous his offence, no Brahman may in Nepal suffer capital punishment; the traditions which still colour Indian life so profoundly in the matter of the sanctity of the cow are represented in this country by reckoning the killing of that animal as a crime equal to the murder of a man; still, as much as ever, religion and religious prejudice and preference attend a man throughout his life from his birth to his funeral. To this day in India a man who loses his caste by infringing its cardinal regulations is sometimes permitted to remain unmolested within its fold by the connivance of the priest. In Nepal however there is no escape.

Not only is there diversity of practice in different parts of India, but the castes themselves conform to no common type. Some are functional, i.e. they have a common occupation

1 *Essays relating to Indian Subjects* (1880), vol. II, p. 241.

or handicraft, as, for instance, goldsmiths, potters, barbers and washermen. The last are of particularly low estate because they handle soiled clothes. So low is the estimation in which they are held that in one part of the country even the Doms, who as scavengers rank even lower, have an oath: "If I do this, may I be like a man who has taken food from a washerman". Both barbers and washermen owe their existence as social units to a state of society very unlike that of Europe: Hindus as a rule neither shave themselves nor wash their own clothes. There are also curious survivals of an earlier age, such as the caste of Bhats, who are both genealogists and bards. They maintain the genealogies of families belonging to their *clientèle*, going from one to another to record births. The family trees often fill bulky tomes: some maintained for a section of Rajputs in the United Province are so massive as to require camels to carry them. The Bhats also compose and recite verses of interminable length at weddings and other family festivals recounting the achievements of the family and extolling the deeds of ancestors.

Some castes, such as the Lingayats of West and South India, have a common cult but no common occupation, and may be classed as sectarian. Originally a sect, which rejected the caste system and the sacerdotal authority of Brahmans, the Lingayats became a caste and are now subdivided into sections which claim recognition as distinct castes. Others are tribal in origin, such as castes composed of the descendants of aboriginals who have been admitted *en masse* into the fold of Hinduism, a tribe being converted into a caste. The usual process is for an aboriginal tribe to set up a Hindu god, get a Hindu priest to minister to them, and adopt some Hindu customs, after which they are recognized as low caste Hindus. Some of a more martial character have been recognized as Kshattriyas or Rajputs. In this way the Kshattriyas of the Manipur State in Assam came into existence early in the eighteenth century. Manipur was at that time ruled over by a Naga chief of Mongoloid origin, who was converted to Hinduism by a wandering ascetic, and his subjects followed suit. The Nagas in their unreclaimed state were bloodthirsty savages, but the Hindu missionary ingeniously declared that they were descended from the hero Arjuna by a Naga woman and were therefore Kshattriyas, who had forgotten their religion and their caste. Another caste which is also known by the name of one of Manu's *varnas* is that of the Sudras of Eastern Bengal and of Sylhet in Assam, which has a very different origin, for it is composed of the descendants of the household slaves of Brahmans and Kayasths.

Some castes again are produced by fission.

The Muchi in North India, who are shoemakers and handle only dressed leather, are distinct from the Chamars, who skin animals and handle raw hides. Other castes start by being a refuge for outcastes, e.g. those who have lost caste by eating forbidden food in times of famine. Even these castes have their sub-castes. In one Bihar district the Kallars (from *kal*, meaning famine) are divided into two sections, of which one lost its original caste in the famine of 1866 and the other ten years later. In Orissa the Chattrakhais are descendants of those who lost caste because during the famine of 1866 they ate in relief kitchens (*chhatra*, whence the name). This caste includes two sub-castes, between which there is no intermarriage, one consisting of those who were originally members of the Brahman and other high castes, the other of men who belonged to lower castes. In Assam, again, the Mekuris account for their origin and name, which means a cat, by a story that they were outcasted because their ancestors inadvertently ate some food into which a cat had dropped a Moslem's food. The legend may seem strange to a European but is quite an intelligible explanation of origin to a Hindu. Even during the War, when Indian troops were on active service, care had to be taken to keep the food of Moslem and Hindu sepoys separate, and on one occasion a complaint that the flies from a Moslem butchery settled on meat prepared for Hindus led to the two slaughter-houses being moved farther apart.[1]

The formation of new castes is not so common as that of sub-castes within a caste. The creation of new sub-castes is due to several causes. Sometimes it is caused by migration to different parts of the country; sub-castes have often territorial designations which show how they came into being. Sometimes a new sub-caste is brought into existence by the adoption of a religious cult: as Sir Alfred Lyall has said, "sects always tend to become sub-castes".[2] This has been the fate of the sect founded by a weaver, Kabir, early in the fifteenth century. Like other reforming sects the Kabirpanthis, as his followers were called, began by abolishing caste distinctions, but ended by recognizing them—a typical example of how much stronger caste is than sect. The Kabirpanthis are now merely sub-castes of different castes, distinguished from other sub-castes by being vegetarians and teetotallers.

Sub-castes are also formed by the adoption of new and (it is believed) reformed customs such as are followed by higher castes. A section of a low caste may claim a higher status and become a separate sub-caste because it forbids the remarriage of widows, another because it adopts the practice of child marriage, a third because it

[1] E. Candler, *The Sepoy* (1919), pp. 130–1.
[2] *Asiatic Studies* (1884), p. 6.

affects a certain nicety about food. Another common cause is the adoption of new occupations. One section of a caste having taken up an occupation which is considered more respectable than those followed by other members of the caste, claims superiority on that account, refuses to let its women marry men belonging to other sections, and becomes a separate sub-caste. There have also been cases in which the adoption of more dignified occupations has enabled sub-castes to join other castes of a better status.

It is sometimes said that a Hindu is born, not made, that consequently no outsider can be admitted to a Hindu caste and that no one can change his caste. These statements are not quite correct. Hindu castes living in proximity to non-Aryan tribes receive as members new converts to Hinduism. Sir James Lyall wrote in the *Kangra Settlement Report*: "On the border line in the Himalayas, between Tibet and India proper, any one can observe caste growing before his eyes; the noble is changing into a Rajput, the priest into a Brahman, the peasant into a Jat, and so on down to the bottom of the scale". In some areas where there is no sharp dividing line between certain castes, men whose power or means are equal to their ambition may succeed in raising themselves to higher castes. In Orissa the Chasas, a clean Sudra caste of agriculturists, admit outsiders, and well-to-do men who are

Chasas by birth are sometimes admitted to membership of the Karan caste (a twice-born caste corresponding to the Kayasths of North India) and assume the Karan title of Mahanti. This custom has given rise to a popular proverb: "Rising, rising to Mahanti, falling, falling to Chasa"; another proverb, which satirizes unfounded claims to membership of the Karan caste, is: "He who has no caste calls himself Mahanti".

Some low castes have no objection to receiving as members men who have been expelled from higher castes. The Bauris of Bengal, to mention one case, commonly have accessions of men who have been expelled from higher castes for eating rice cooked by their Bauri mistresses. All that the entrant has to do is to pay his footing by means of a donation, which is spent at a caste feast, at which he eats for the first time with his new associates.

Chapter II

CASTE GOVERNMENT

THERE is a saying in Northern India *Jāt kā rājā jāt*, meaning "The caste is its own ruler". This assertion of autonomy is based on fact, for each caste is a self-governing community. It regulates its affairs and enforces its unwritten law independently of others and, except in the cases mentioned in the next chapter, enjoys freedom from outside control including that of the Brahmans.

Much has been written about the domination of Hindu society by the Brahmans, and there is no question of the theocratic power which they exercise by reason of their position as a sacrosanct order and as the intermediaries between the gods and men. But their authority, vast as it is, does not supersede or overrule that of the caste. It rests with the caste itself to decide who its members shall be and, by regulations as to their manner of life, to determine what shall be the conditions of membership.

The caste is the custodian of its own laws. It punishes those who offend against them and restores penitents to caste in independence of the Brahmans, though not without consulting them when offences have been committed which have to be expiated by ceremonies of a religious nature. The function of the Brahmans is to officiate at ceremonies and, when consulted, to declare what actions have or have not scriptural sanction and what expiations are required by the Hindu scriptures or tradition. In this way they may advise as to a fitting punishment when the caste itself has come to a verdict of guilty; but they cannot compel a caste to follow their advice or take any particular course of action. The limitation of their authority in this respect has been well explained by Dr Ketkar in dealing with the hypothetical case of a convert to Christianity who wishes to revert to Hinduism and consequently to be readmitted to his old caste.

> In this case the proper authority to appeal to is the representatives of his own old caste. Appeal to the Hindu community in general or to Brahmans is useless. It is unnecessary first of all, and secondly, if it is done, it would not bring about the desired results. All that the Brahmans can do is to purify the individual by giving him some sort of penance, but they cannot make him a member of any definite caste. The caste decides for itself as to who its members should be.[1]

At the same time the Brahmans can and do exercise considerable influence because of their sacerdotal functions. They are required to officiate at certain ceremonies, especially on the

[1] *An Essay on Hinduism* (1911), p. 70.

occasion of births, deaths and marriages; and refusal to officiate is a powerful weapon for the punishment of any one of whose conduct they disapprove.

For the purposes of self-government the lower castes are far better organized than the higher, which rarely have any machinery for the regulation of their affairs. The lower castes, on the other hand, have, as a rule, a very effective organization for making and enforcing their decrees. Caste government among them is implemented by governing bodies and headmen to whom authority is delegated. The constitution of the governing bodies varies. Sometimes it is a general assembly of the adult male members of the caste, all of whom have a right of admission to, and free utterance in, meetings. Sometimes it is a council composed of heads of houses or of representatives of families, who hold office by hereditary right or by appointment for life: in the latter case the members of the caste elect to vacancies as they occur. A special council may also be constituted *ad hoc* for the settlement of some particular question or the adjudication of a special case, after the decision of which its powers lapse. In some cases again the management of caste affairs is vested in the headman of the caste, but this is somewhat rare, the headman generally acting in association with permanent councils.

The commonest kind of caste council is that

which consists of the elder men of the caste, recognized leaders who command the respect and confidence of their community. This forms a kind of standing committee under the presidentship of the headman. In the trial of offenders against caste rules its members act like a jury with the headman as a presiding judge; in matters of common interest to the caste it is like the directorate of a company. Ordinarily it deals with all caste questions arising within its jurisdiction, and its permanence and authority do much to promote the solidarity of the caste and to preserve discipline among its members; but for matters of grave and general importance it may give place to a general assembly of the male members of the caste: even then the members of the council guide the discussion and have a large voice in the final decision.

Whatever may be its constitution, the governing body is commonly known as a *panchāyat*, which means literally a body of five men. In practice there is no such fixation of numbers, and the term is applied to an indefinite number of men. As an institution the *panchāyat* or representative assembly is held in peculiar esteem, which is expressed by the popular saying: "The voice of the *panchāyat* is the voice of God". This saying is not confined to the caste *panchāyat*, but is used generally of representative bodies which deal with communal affairs. As it is convenient to have a single term to cover the different kinds of governing bodies, they may be referred to generically as caste councils.

It must not be imagined that a whole caste is governed by one council. On the contrary, there are different councils for different sections of a caste, because only those who can intermarry can have a common council, and, as stated in the last chapter, there is as a rule no intermarriage between the sub-castes. A caste will therefore have one common council only in the rare cases in which there are no sub-castes. Questions of marriage customs and breaches of the marriage law are the most important matters coming within the purview of the caste council; and each sub-caste administers its own marriage law. The circle for which a caste council is constituted is further defined by the rules as to eating together, for those who cannot eat together cannot have a common council. Communal feasts are a common feature of caste government; when a general meeting is held, a feast is the usual finale; and offenders against the caste laws are frequently fined by having to pay for a feast, in which they join, thus symbolizing their readmission to fellowship. Actually, however, the deciding factor is intermarriage, for those who may intermarry may eat and drink together.

While, however, the caste councils are limited in this way to those who can intermarry and who can eat and drink together, these can also be general conclaves of all members of a caste for the consideration of questions affecting all the sub-castes. This, however, is a special meeting summoned for a special purpose, and it is quite distinct from the ordinary caste councils: cases of a thousand men gathering together at such a meeting are not unknown. Different caste councils also occasionally combine when there is any grave matter of general interest to decide upon, as, for example, when one local community having outcasted a man, another receives him in communion, and a general meeting is required to settle the difference between them.

The actual unit over which a caste council has jurisdiction is determined by practical considerations, such as the numerical strength of the caste in any particular locality, the number of villages which it inhabits, and their distance apart. The government of a caste, like that of a country, depends largely on communications. If the members of a caste are concentrated in a small area, they have one council; if they are scattered over a considerable area, there are several, each with a defined local jurisdiction. There may, therefore, according to circumstances, be one council for a single village or ward of a town, or there may be one for a group of villages or wards.

Not uncommonly also there is a regular gradation of caste councils, those constituted for a small area being subordinate to others which control a large area. When this is the case, there is often a well-defined representative system, the superior councils being elected by those below them and settling questions beyond the competence of the latter. Among the Iluvans of Tinnevelly each village has its own council and elects two representatives to a council which controls a union of villages. Each group of five to seven union councils elects five members to a divisional council, which exercises authority over the *nādu* (division or tract of country). In the same way among the Panikhans of Madras eleven villages form a union, on the council of which each village has a representative, and eleven unions form a *nādu* and elect the members of its council. In some parts of North India the superior councils have names suggesting the number of villages forming the union over which it has authority, such as Bargaon, Bawan and Chaurasi, meaning twelve, fifty-two and eighty respectively. It does not follow that these are the exact number of the villages in each union; the numbers are expressive of quantity rather than definitive.

The executive consists of two or three office-bearers. By far the most important is the headman, who presides at meetings of the caste council and has the authority which his designation implies. Next in rank is a man who presides over meetings in the absence of the headman. The third functionary is a subordinate, a kind of beadle, who acts as the headman's messenger, summons meetings, and collects the fines imposed by the council. The headman and beadle are found almost invariably, the vice-president is not so common. In some castes these offices are held for life, and when an incumbent dies, the men of the caste elect his successor. More generally they are hereditary: if one of them devolves on a minor or on a person who for any reason is incapable of discharging its duties, another member of his family may act in his place. In one caste, the Kultas of Sambalpur in Orissa, where the headmanship is hereditary, women have been known to succeed to the office, but this is a solitary exception to the rule that men only can be headmen.

As with the councils, so with the headmen, there are in some areas and among some castes gradations of jurisdiction. In the Trichinopoly district, for example, there are superior headmen who have authority over a number of groups of villages, each of which has its own headman. They act as an appellate or revisional authority, if the local councils are unable to come to a decision, or if their decisions are disputed. In one Bihar district a sub-caste of Goalas has so far copied the official system and nomenclature that it has a headman with jurisdiction over the whole district who rejoices in the English title of Judge. The headman in some castes enjoys certain privileges. In one section of the Vellalans of Tinnevelly he is given a seat on a dais at meetings, at which everyone else has to stand, and consequently enjoys the quaint title of Irunkol, meaning "Please sit down". In another caste he is given a gold ring to wear and is humbly saluted with folded hands—a form of obeisance. In a third he has the right to ride on horseback and to use an umbrella, privileges which the ordinary man does not enjoy, besides which any man of the caste coming before him prostrates himself.

The position of the headman is not only one of honour, but also of considerable authority: among some castes in the Central Provinces, even when the headman happens to be a child (as may be the case if the post is hereditary in a particular family), the decision of the caste council is submitted to him as a matter of form for ratification.[1] As a rule he does not act independently of the council, except in petty cases; but a man of wealth and influence may sometimes acquire a monopoly of power and act like a dictator without the assistance or concurrence of any council. In some parts of South India

[1] *Central Provinces Census Report for 1911*, Part I, p. 389.

and among some castes, the headman is like a chief with practically absolute power. Such is the case among the Maravans of Madras, whose headmen, besides deciding on cases of breaches of caste rules, have a peculiar duty due to the fact that the Maravans are a caste of criminal propensities. From them the village watchmen are drawn, on the principle either of setting a thief to catch a thief or of employing one as security against the misconduct of his fellows. The watchman's task is not merely to detect thefts but to prevent them; and if a theft occurs, the Maravans of the village have to make good the loss. Their headman then acts as an arbiter, for he apportions the amount to be paid by each family as compensation to the victims of the theft. The system does not work too well, for in order to compensate one householder the watchman will himself commit theft from another, or he will give a promissory note for the value of the stolen property which he has no intention of redeeming.

The functions of the caste councils are mainly judicial, and to a minor degree deliberative and legislative, i.e. they mostly act as tribunals for the trial of offences against caste rules, though they also discuss and decide questions affecting the customs and interests of the caste and formulate rules of conduct. The headman may summon a meeting on receipt of a complaint that a member of the caste has committed a breach of caste rules; or a man who is suspected of, or has been charged with, an offence may ask for one to be called together in order that he may clear himself. The latter is particularly the case when, a man being under suspicion, his caste fellows cut off communion with him. If he has any case to put forward, it is to his interest to meet, and, if possible, to rebut the charge as soon as he can. Sometimes also a charge is preferred impromptu when the members of the caste are already assembled for some common purpose, such as a dinner or feast; an inquiry is then held on the spot.

Except when this is the case, the headman has a meeting of the caste council summoned, the messenger being sent round to give notice of time and place. Among some castes the summons takes a curious form. In one part of Bengal the messengers of the Kumhar or potter caste take round leaves of the betel leaf plant called *pān* (*Piper betel*), and are consequently known as Pan-patras (from *pān* and *patrā*, a letter); in Bihar one caste uses areca nuts (with which *pān* is usually chewed) for the same purpose. In the Central Provinces a twig serves as a missive among certain aboriginal tribes; and, on the other hand, some castes are modern enough in their ways to have summonses sent by post in areas where post-offices are handy.

The procedure is simple. The charge having been stated, the accused is questioned. If he admits his guilt, sentence follows. If he denies the charge, witnesses are heard in support of the accusation and in defence, after which comes the verdict. If the charge is shown to be false and malicious, the accuser receives prompt and condign punishment. He may be outcasted for a time or fined or subjected to corporal punishment: sometimes he will be kicked by every member of the council, sometimes bound hand and foot or tied up in a mat for some hours. When an offence appears to be of a religious character, Brahmans may be referred to for a ruling as to its nature and the expiation required. This is commonly done when a man is charged with having caused the death of a cow by neglect, carelessness, or ill-treatment. In Orissa there is an expert in such cases, who is called in when there is a suspected case of cow-killing. He is versed in the ordinances about the treatment of cows and advises whether the death is tantamount to cow-killing, and if so, what expiation should be exacted. In ordinary cases, however, the caste considers itself quite competent to come to a decision and to pass sentence.

Evidence is frequently given on oath. The witnesses swear by Ganges water, the sacred *tulsi* plant, and copper, or by the cow (holding the tail of one), or by the head of one of their sons. The accused may also take an oath of his innocence, invoking dreadful penalties in case of his guilt or perjury, e.g. that he will be struck blind or his children will die within a certain time. A man who is really guilty is generally so afraid of the awful consequences that he shrinks from the oath, and the inference is clear.

In some parts an air of religious solemnity is imparted to the proceedings by the trial being held in a temple or by requiring the accused to take an oath in a temple. One Brahman sub-caste in Sambalpur has a curious form of procedure. The accused has to take an oath in a temple of special sanctity, and its terms are recorded on a palm-leaf: writing on palm-leaves is a very ancient practice in Orissa. The oath is of the usual tenor, e.g. that if guilty, he will become blind or his children will die in a specified time, such as three days, weeks or months. The leaf is kept in the temple for the period named, and the accused is temporarily outcasted pending the establishment of his innocence. If at the end of the time he and his family have suffered no evil, he reappears before the caste council with the palm-leaf, and applies for readmission to communion with the caste. This is a refined form of trial by ordeal.

Actual trials by ordeal of a primitive kind are occasionally resorted to by more primitive communities in backward areas as a solution in cases of doubt, e.g. the accused may be required to put a hand into boiling oil or to carry in his hand a piece of red-hot metal.

The proceedings are almost invariably oral, but occasionally a record is made, if the members of the caste are literate enough and if there is likely to be a case in the law courts. In one district caste councils have so far copied the procedure of the law courts that, when grave charges are made, they frequently require the complaint to be written out and the complainant's thumb impression to be affixed to it.

The matters which come before the caste council are for the most part offences connected with marriage and morals, food and drink, smoking with men of other castes, and prohibited occupations. Their number is legion, for they also comprise breaches of etiquette and even the amenities of private life, as well as patent breaches of custom or the unwritten law of the caste, of which the nature will be realized from the account given in subsequent chapters. The caste councils further deal with religious offences, such as the omission, or the improper performance, of rites at ceremonies, like marriages and funerals, and the killing, or causing the death of, sacred animals and birds. The commonest cases under the latter head are connected with the deaths of cows owing to want of proper treatment or care on the part of their owners, e.g. if they are strangled by a rope round the neck while in a stall. To kill a cow deliberately and by one's own act is almost unheard of, except among the most degraded castes having only a faint veneer of Hinduism; but men are sometimes impelled by penury or greed to sell a cow to a butcher. This is almost as heinous an offence as the direct slaughtering of the animal and is visited by the severest penalties. Associated with religion also are a number of miscellaneous offences connected with pollution, such as contact with a dead animal, the handling of hides or leather, and even being beaten with shoes. The same idea of uncleanness seems to underlie the punishments imposed by some castes for the peculiarly offensive state of having maggots in a wound or sore.

Not every little matter comes before the caste councils. The headmen and elders often settle disputes out of court, effect compromises, and reprimand petty offenders without the formality of a trial. The councils themselves do a good deal of non-judicial work. They arrange for the partition of property among members of families which have decided to separate, enforce both the fulfilment of promises of marriage and the restoration of runaway wives, and determine the maintenance to be given to divorced women—the last a rare contingency. In addition, they allot such common funds as the caste may have either from the realization of fines or from the collection of subscriptions from members of the caste.

The funds are used for religious or charitable purposes, for works of public utility, and for common entertainments and incidental expenses. Assignments are made for the maintenance of temples, and one may be built if there is sufficient money. Wells and tanks are constructed to furnish a supply of drinking water. Grants are made for the support of the poor and the education of orphans, or to enable a poor family to meet the expenses of a marriage or of funeral ceremonies: alms and food are given to Brahmans as well as destitute members of the caste. Occasionally money is provided for litigation in which the interests of the local community are affected. Perhaps the commonest way of spending the money accumulated from fines is the provision of common feasts and the purchase of mats, pots and pitchers to be used at them.

The caste councils exercise a close control over the members of their community and keep up a pretty strict discipline. The limits for which they are constituted are small enough for neighbours to know fairly accurately all that goes on, and the caste is prompt to act on the slightest suspicion of conduct which is improper from its own point of view. Relations with the suspect are at once cut off, and he is boycotted until he clears himself. This is specially the case in the villages and among the lower castes. The lower the caste, the stricter it is in enforcing caste rules and preserving the honour of the caste. When a caste council has passed orders, contumacy is rare. The council has the whip hand, for, if a man refuses to bow to its sentence and defies its authority, he is outcasted until he makes his submission.

Occasionally, however, the caste may be divided over the question of a man's guilt, or a man may be sufficiently influential to be able to defy his inquisitors. In the *Madras Census Report of 1911* Mr Molony mentioned the case of a Brahman who was abandoned enough to eat beef and drink forbidden liquors; but he knew the law of libel and could pay for witnesses to depose on his behalf. The caste could do nothing to him until his death. Then it took its revenge, for no one could be got, for love or money, to carry his corpse to the funeral pyre.

The law courts have had a considerable influence on the system of caste government. The lawyer is abroad in India, as well as the schoolmaster, and the authority of the caste councils is affected by the knowledge which even the villager has of his legal remedies. Caste councils are chary of dealing with a charge if there is a danger that a man whom they punish may bring a case, e.g. of defamation, against them. Sometimes, indeed, this happens and they are put on their trial. The council, however, can play the same game and have a case got up in the courts against an intransigeant culprit. Sometimes, too, a council abdicates its functions if it considers the case too serious or difficult for its own adjudication, and refers the parties to the courts.

Caste councils occasionally agree to cases being brought in the courts by way of appeal from their orders, but as a rule they resent any reference being made either to the magistrates or the police in matters which fall within their own prerogative. In such cases they bring pressure to bear on the complainant to make him or her withdraw the case, and they punish those who persist in legal proceedings. As an instance in point, a woman complained to the police, truly enough, that a man of her caste had attempted to ravish her. The council took the matter up, outcasted the man for six months, and got the woman to withdraw the charge on pain of a similar punishment.

There is quite commonly a conspiracy of silence when the interests of a casteman are at stake in the law courts. Witnesses against him are not forthcoming, and if some one has the hardihood to depose, he is heavily requited for doing so. As a magistrate in India, I heard two cases within a few weeks, which illustrate this. Both were cases of murder; in both the victim was a young widow who had strayed from the paths of virtue; and, curiously enough, both women had the same name, though they were of different castes. The first was a Rajput woman, who had an intrigue with a brother of her deceased husband. The other brothers murdered her as a punishment, and not a scrap of evidence could be obtained from any Rajput, for all considered that she deserved her fate. The other was a woman of low caste, and the only evidence against the accused was that of her son, a little boy who had been an eyewitness of the murder. He was outcasted for deposing against his caste fellows and would have been left utterly destitute had not a kind-hearted policeman adopted him. One exception to this rule should be mentioned. If a man is a nuisance to his neighbours, or such a bad character that there is no hope of reformation as a result of caste action, his fellow-castemen are only too glad to get him put into prison, and will give evidence against him with alacrity.

It has been observed that in India the spirit of combination is always in the inverse ratio to the rank of the class, weakest in the highest, and strongest in the lowest class.[1] This is certainly true of castes; the high castes seldom have any organization such as is found among the lower

[1] Sir W. H. Sleeman, *Rambles and Recollections of an Indian Official* (edited by V. A. Smith) (1915), p. 50.

castes. There is rarely any one with authority to take the initiative in case of complaints, or any governing body to take offenders to task or try them and pass judgment on them. If there is an open and flagrant scandal, the caste will by common consent cut off relations with the offender, or the more influential members of the community may hold an informal meeting to discuss the matter and decide what attitude they should adopt. It is hard, however, to get the higher castes to take a common course of action, and their control over their members is by no means close and effective. Consequently they have neither the same solidarity nor the same power to enforce social and moral discipline as those lower in the scale. One section of a caste may ostracize a man who has committed, or is suspected of, a breach of caste or religious usages, another may continue to receive him in communion. We are told that when Mr Gandhi returned to his home at Rajkot after his first visit to England, "he was duly received back into communion with the members of his caste. Meanwhile the leaders of his caste in Bombay and Porbandar had regularly excommunicated him, and to this day Mahatma Gandhi is excluded by them from religious privileges".[1]

Men of wealth and position are often able

1 R. M. Gray and Manilal C. Parekh, *Mahatma Gandhi: An Essay in Appreciation* (1924), pp. 8–9.

to defy those who seek to ostracize them. They enlist friends and sympathizers, and a caste is not infrequently split by faction, as in a case (mentioned in the *Madras Census Report of 1911*) in which a man, who had been excommunicated for a voyage overseas, gathered a party round him and formed a society which excommunicated his excommunicators.

The absence of regularly constituted and recognized tribunals for the trial of offences has one distinct disadvantage. A man may be excommunicated without full inquiry and without any possibility of being heard in his defence. There is no appeal possible against the tacit verdict of a community, and a man who has been outcasted has therefore little prospect of restoration to caste. On the other hand, the want of system insures more individual liberty. The higher castes rarely trouble about the petty matters which exercise the lower. They generally take cognizance only of cases in which men return from voyages overseas, of breaches of the marriage laws, such as the remarriage of widows and open immorality (more particularly among women), and, to a less extent, eating and drinking forbiddden food or sharing meals with men of other castes.

The more highly educated members of the high castes themselves appreciate the liberty which they enjoy by not being in tutelage to any central authority. At a conference which one advanced community held in Bombay some years ago a proposal to revive caste *panchāyats* or councils met with determined opposition. It was maintained that individual liberty and scope for development were essential to progress, and the revival of the authority of the councils was denounced as the greatest of evils.[1]

[1] *Bombay Census Report for 1911*, Part I, p. 201.

Chapter III

EXTERNAL CONTROL

THE claim of the castes to have the right to manage their affairs without any control from outside finds no sanction in early Hindu writings. On the contrary, these invested the king with special authority in social matters. He was charged with the duty of seeing that each of the four *varnas* or orders mentioned in Chapter I performed its proper functions, and it was incumbent on him to punish those who ventured to leave their allotted sphere. The Brahmans were to declare what their respective functions were, the king was to govern them accordingly. In other words, civil was to support spiritual authority, and the secular power to enforce ecclesiastical decrees.

Apart from the injunctions of the law books, there is no doubt that the king actually exercised considerable authority in caste matters. He issued marriage regulations for castes, he fixed the social rank of different sub-castes, he promoted members of one caste to another, and he degraded them to a lower. According to tradition, Ballal Sen, King of Bengal, in the twelfth century, determined by royal warrant the precedence of different sections of the Brahmans in his territories, raised the status of three castes, and degraded a fourth, a trading caste, which he declared to be an unclean caste, for which Brahmans could not officiate without themselves losing status. In the early part of the fourteenth century, again, Raja Hara Singh Deva, who was first the ruler of a principality in North Bihar and afterwards a king in Nepal, settled the respective ranks of three sections of the Maithil sub-caste of Brahmans and made marriage rules for them; and it should be noted that he was not a Brahman but a Kshattriya.

To come to more recent times, the Peshwas, who ruled over the Marathas during the eighteenth century, were the final authority for the Chitpavan Brahmans, and also to a certain extent for other castes in their dominions, in questions of religious observance and social custom. According to Dr Ketkar, any decision of the Peshwas' Council was unchallenged from Benares to Rameshwaram, i.e. through the greater part of India; "but", he adds, "the days of the Peshwas are gone, unfortunately to return no more".[1]

The Rajput rulers in the Kangra Hills of the Punjab, who held independent power there until the nineteenth century, also had effectual authority in caste matters, and made a classification of grades of Brahmans (doubtless on the

[1] *An Essay on Hinduism* (1911), pp. 82–3.

advice of Brahmans) which was binding on all Brahmans in their territory. Sir James Lyall (afterwards Lieutenant-Governor of the Punjab) wrote in the *Kangra Settlement Report*:

> Till lately the limits of caste do not seem to have been so immutably fixed in the hills as in the plains. The Raja was the fountain of honour and could do much as he liked. I have heard old men quote instances within their memory in which a Raja promoted a Girth [Ghirath] to be a Rathi and a Thakur to be a Rajput for services done or money given; and at the present day the power of admitting back into caste fellowship persons put under a ban for some grave act of defilement is a source of income to the Jagirdar Rajas.[1]

Other instances of the exercise of the royal prerogative in caste matters are given in Sir Denzil Ibbetson's *Panjab Castes*, where it is stated that the Raja of Kangra was bribed to elevate one particular caste, and that the Raja of Alwar made a new caste from a section of an old one and prescribed limits to intermarriage between members of the new and old castes.

The power of the Rajput princes was swept away in the plains when their territories were brought under Moslem rule, and Sir Denzil Ibbetson has propounded the view that the Muhammadan conquest strengthened rather

[1] Loc. cit. Sir Denzil Ibbetson, *Panjab Castes* (Lahore, 1916), p. 7.

than relaxed the bonds of caste by depriving the Hindu population of their natural leaders, the Rajputs, and throwing them into the hands of the Brahmans, who took their place. The case was very different in the Kangra Hills. There the Hindu Rajas, though often attacked, were never subdued, and their principalities remained a stronghold both of Rajput power and of Hinduism under Rajput, and not Brahman, control. Secure in their hilly fastnesses many Rajput families continued to exercise the royal power in caste as in other matters, and degradation from and elevation to Rajput rank were in the hands of the Raja, who was thus the arbiter of caste.[1]

The Moslem rulers, looking down on the Hindus as idolatrous heathens, left them to settle caste questions as they pleased; their attitude was as detached as that of Gallio; but the Mughal Government in Bengal, during the eighteenth century at least, reserved to itself the right to sanction readmission to caste,[2] and on its downfall the British inherited the same preroga-

[1] *Panjab Castes* (Lahore, 1916), pp. 15–16, 101.

[2] See the subsequent quotation from Verelst's *View of the English Government in Bengal* (1772). Mr S. C. Bose, in *The Hindus as they are* (Calcutta, 1883, p. 167), mentions the case of a Brahman family which had been outcasted appealing in vain to the Mughal Nawab of Bengal for restoration to caste. A refusal to sanction reinstatement in caste was calculated to drive an outcaste into the fold of Islam.

tive. It was stated in the instructions drafted in 1769 for Supervisors, i.e. British officers placed in charge of the revenue administration in Bengal:

> When any man has naturally forfeited his cast (*sic*), you are to observe that he cannot be restored to it without the sanction of Government; which was a political supremacy reserved to themselves by the Mahomedans, and which, as it publicly asserts the subordination of Hindoos, who are so considerable a majority of subjects, ought not to be laid down; though every indulgence and privilege of caste should be otherwise allowed them.[1]

Elsewhere Verelst, who was Governor of Bengal from 1767 to 1769, explained that as the punishment of degradation from caste depended upon the opinion of the people themselves, it could not be inflicted by the English Governor

> unless the mandate of a Governor could instantly change the religious sentiments of a nation. Neither can a man once degraded be restored but by the general suffrage of his own tribe, the sanction of the Bramins (who are the head tribe) and the superadded concurrence of the supreme civil power.[2]

The power which was thus claimed for Government was waived in the same year on the very proper ground that there was no longer the

[1] H. Verelst, *View of the English Government in Bengal* (1772), p. 238 (Appendix).

[2] *Ibid.* p. 28 (note).

necessity of publicly asserting the subordination of Hindus to Moslems.[1] In the town of Calcutta, however, a regular court, known as the Caste Cutcherry (court), was for some time maintained by the British for the settlement of caste questions. The British Governor was nominally its president: the *de facto* president was his Indian Banyan or agent, whom he deputed to act for him. Warren Hastings stated: "I myself am President, but I conceive myself merely a name to authenticate the acts of others". The Caste Cutcherry had, he said, cognizance of disputes only among the lower classes of Hindus, and his Banyan presided over it "by virtue of the immemorial usage of the settlement", in the same way that every other Banyan of the Governor had done.[2] Long-established precedent did not save Warren Hastings from being attacked on this point by Burke. With characteristic exaggeration Burke declared that the banyans of Warren Hastings, Krishna Kanta Das (Cantoo Baboo) and Ganga Gobinda Singh, whom he had placed over the Caste Cutcherry, "had the caste and character of all the people of Bengal in their hands" and were enthroned on

[1] See Dr J. Wise, "The Muhammadans of Eastern Bengal", *Journal of the Asiatic Society of Bengal*, 1894, Part III, p. 30.

[2] See G. W. Forrest, *Selections from State Papers 1772–1785* (1890), vol. II, p. 367.

"the first seat of ecclesiastical jurisdiction, which was to decide upon the castes of all those people, including their rank, their family, their honour, their happiness here, and, in their judgment, their salvation hereafter".

Some individual instances have also been recorded of British officers in Madras setting aside the authority of caste representatives in the early years of the nineteenth century. In Coimbatore a Major Macleod superseded hereditary headmen and ordered that cases of caste offences should be heard by a tahsildar (an Indian officer of Government), assisted by an assembly of the most respectable men of the castes concerned. The tahsildar, after consulting the assembly as to the customs of the castes, passed sentence. Any one who refused to submit to the decision of the tahsildar and assembly was immediately banished from the district. Major Macleod was himself beloved by the people and had no difficulty in securing the restoration to caste rights of those who had been deprived of them by the spite or caprice of the headman. Another officer in Coimbatore, finding that the headmen of a certain caste exercised their authority unjustly, similarly ordered all caste questions to be settled in the public court by a tahsildar with the advice of a caste council, to the satisfaction of the people themselves.[1]

[1] F. Buchanan, *A Journey from Madras through the countries of Mysore, Canara and Malabar* (1807), vol. II, pp. 294, 329.

There is no official control of caste and no State interference with caste customs in British India. The Government follows a policy of non-intervention, for it is a fixed principle that it should not interfere with social laws and personal customs unless there is a general and unequivocal demand for reform on the part of the people themselves. Yet such is the force of immemorial tradition that the castes expect the British Government to exercise the prerogative of the ancient Hindu kings by prescribing the social status of castes. At each recurring census the census authorities are inundated by memorials from different castes petitioning Government to recognize their claim to a higher rank than they are actually accorded by the Hindu community at large. It is a curious link with the past that they are particularly anxious to be acknowledged as belonging to two *varnas* or orders of Manu, the Kshattriyas and Vaisyas. Government, however, steadfastly declines to intervene or to assume any control over caste matters.

It is far otherwise in Nepal, which prides itself on being a well of Hinduism pure and undefiled. There the castes are to a certain extent under State control; for the courts of law adjudicate on cases involving either expulsion from a caste and degradation from a higher to a lower caste; the Prime Minister himself is the final court of appeal. Minor delinquencies are punished by the caste councils; and the courts take cognizance only of heinous offences, such as the killing of cows and cases in which members of different caste have illicit relations. When the woman's caste is the higher, she is degraded to the level of her lover; when the man's caste is the higher, he is similarly degraded if he takes cooked rice or *dāl* (pulses) from his mistress: if, however, he merely keeps her, and does not eat food cooked or served by her, he can retain his caste. The caste to which the offspring of such a union is to bc allotted is also determined by the courts. In addition to excommunication and degradation, the courts inflict civil penalties for caste offences, and their sentences are apt to be severe. For instance, a man had an intrigue with a low caste woman with the connivance of a headman. The guilty lover was degraded to the caste of his paramour; so also was the headman; and all three were imprisoned for seven years. It is not surprising that Brian Houghton Hodgson wrote:

> It is in Nepal alone, of all Hindu States, that two-thirds of the time of the judges is employed in the discussion of cases better fitted for the confessional, or the tribunal of public opinion, or some domestic court, such as the *Panchāyet* of brethren or fellow-craftsmen, than for a King's court of justice.[1]

In the Protected States of India few chiefs have

[1] See *Essays relating to Indian Subjects* (1880), vol. II, pp. 239–40.

retained their position as the paramount caste authority to such an extent as the chiefs of the Feudatory States of Orissa, a tract long isolated and untouched by modernizing influences. The castes have their own councils, but in almost every case the headman is appointed by the chief. Ordinarily the caste councils settle the cases brought before them, but the chief intervenes in two classes of cases, viz. disputes which a caste council is unable to settle and appeals from its orders. Any one dissatisfied with the finding of a caste council has a right of appeal to the chief, whose finding is final. He may either decide a case off-hand or refer it to a kind of jury of Brahmans and other men of standing and esteem, who usually hear it in the chief's temple at the capital of the State. Whatever their finding may be, it has to be submitted for orders to the chief, who may endorse, modify or reject it. He may direct the outcasting of any one, even a Brahman, and any person who disobeys his order by associating with the outcasted man may himself be outcasted. A notable instance of the chief's power in this respect occurred some years ago. A caste, which had not only superior rank but much wealth and influence, was divided into two parties over the question whether one of its young men had had a liaison with a low caste woman. It was eventually decided at a mass meeting of the caste that the suspect was not guilty, and the chief confirmed its finding. The section which was convinced of his guilt refused to accept this verdict and proceeded to treat him as an outcaste. The chief dealt promptly and effectually with the rebellious section. He outcasted every man belonging to it, forbade the priests, barbers and washermen of his State to render them any service, and prevented them getting in any one from outside it. The Political Officer who sent me an account of this incident said that the outcastes were reduced to a pitiable state. They were as a rule clean-shaven, spruce and smart; as a result of the chief's order they had long beards matted with dirt, their hair hung in long strands and was filthy in the extreme, and their clothes were beyond description for uncleanliness.

Sometimes, as, for instance, when a chief is a minor, a State is brought under what is called direct management, i.e. the British Government assumes temporary control of its administration and places a Political Officer in charge of it. This officer takes the place of the Raja as the highest authority in caste matters and in Orissa at any rate is treated with the same respect as the Raja himself. When he enters the State, a deputation of Brahmans receives him with the same honours as the Raja, gives him their benediction, and places powdered sandal-wood on his head. If, however, as sometimes happens, the Political

Officer does not care to exercise the Raja's power as supreme head of the castes, it is apt to lapse, as the minor may follow suit on his accession and not resume this function of his office.

In the Central Provinces the authority of the Chief of the Bastar State is equal to that of the Chiefs of the Orissa Feudatory States. He is a final court of appeal from the orders of caste councils, with a power extending to excommunication; he can also confer the sacred thread on members of the low castes. The Chief of Jashpur in the same province can excommunicate a member of any caste, including even a Brahman, and his order is so effectual that any one who has dealings with a man whom he has expelled from caste suffers the same fate.[1]

In the Himalayan Hill States of the Punjab the Rajas retain in no small degree their ancient prerogatives. The Rajas of the Simla Hill States commonly decide caste disputes, the parties appearing before them accompanied by leading representatives of the castes concerned. The firm belief in the divinity of the ruler, it is said, prevents any attempt to tell a lie.[2] An outcaste in these States cannot be readmitted to caste except with the sanction of the chief, in whose presence the ceremony of expiation takes place. The subordination of caste to the civil power is

[1] *Central Provinces Census Report for 1911*, Part 1, p. 239.

[2] *Punjab Census Report for 1911*, Part 1, p. 427.

marked in Kashmir by the existence of a council, called the Dharma Sabha, which meets in the Maharaja's temple at the capital, Srinagar, and which delivers judgment not only in religious but also in caste matters and deprives men of their castes. The Maharaja himself is acknowledged as head of the Rajput community not only within his own territories (Jammu and Kashmir) but also in adjoining British districts. The Raja of Junga in the Punjab has an authority in certain matters derived from a religious rather than a secular source. Cases in which the conjugal fidelity of women is at issue are brought before him, and he is said to act as the mouthpiece of a god whose temple is situated at Junga, for he announces on behalf of the god whether the women should retain their caste and after what atonement or penalty, if any.[1]

In South India the Raja of Cochin, who is a Kshattriya, acts as an arbiter in caste matters for the Nambudri Brahmans of Malabar.[2] In his own State he can raise anyone from a lower to a higher caste, and no order of complete excommunication can be made except by him or with his sanction.[3]

In the Bombay Presidency references about caste disputes and appeals against the orders of caste councils are made to the Durbars or

[1] *Punjab Census Report for 1911*, Part I, p. 427.

[2] *Madras Census Report for 1911*, Part I, p. 180.

[3] *Cochin Census Report for 1911*, pp. 69, 70.

Governments of the States. In this way the Rajpipla Durbar settled in 1904 a vexed question of hypergamy among the Lewa Kunbis, made regulations as to the areas from which brides should be obtained, and succeeded in reducing the scale of their marriage expenses.[1] The chiefs in Rajputana usually leave the castes to settle their own affairs; but difficulties or differences can be, and sometimes are, referred, at the instance of the castes themselves, either to the Durbar or to the law courts, whose orders are final and embrace the excommunication even of Brahmans. The general tendency is for the chief himself to be the ultimate authority in the small States and for adjudication to be left to the civil courts in the larger States of Rajputana.[2]

Most of the princes of the more important States elsewhere have allowed their power of control over caste to fall into disuse. At Indore and Gwalior there were until comparatively recent times councils composed of Sastris, i.e. men learned in the Hindu law-books. These councils, of which the members were appointed by the ruling prince, decided caste questions and their decisions were final unless the Maharaja overrode them, as he had a right to do and in fact sometimes did. Similarly in Baroda, if any one

[1] *Bombay Census Report for 1911*, Part 1, p. 202.

[2] *Rajputana and Ajmer-Merwara Census Report for 1911*, Part 1, p. 264.

appealed to the Maharaja Gaekwar against any order or decision of a caste council, he referred the case to the President of the State Sastris, who after hearing it submitted it, with his opinion, to the Maharaja Gaekwar for orders. The effect was in many cases that excommunication was commuted to a milder sentence. If a caste refused to accept the finding, it was deprived, by an interdict of the Maharaja Gaekwar, of the services of priests, washermen, and barbers, and was debarred from transactions with grain-dealers and shop-keepers. The Maharaja Gaekwar no longer, however, exercises jurisdiction over any castes except the Marathas, of whom he is the head. Social questions affecting the latter are within the purview of a general committee, which is supervised by a State officer called the Senapati: in 1911 an Englishman held this office. The committee disposes of the questions brought before it, but its decisions are subject to appeal to the Maharaja Gaekwar.

In some parts of India the authority of the caste council is supplemented, and may even be supplanted, by that of the heads of religious orders, as, for instance, by the Gosains in the Brahmaputra Valley of Assam, where the Hindus are chiefly Vaishnavas. The Gosains are the heads of institutions called *Satras*, in which they live with their disciples; the larger correspond to monasteries, as their inmates are celibates;

otherwise they partake of the character of colleges. They are supported from the landed property which they possess and from the offerings of the faithful. The Gosains themselves are held in great reverence and are looked up to as the supreme authorities in social as well as religious matters by thousands of villagers. Caste government is carried on in the usual fashion by the caste councils but doubtful or difficult cases are referred to a Gosain, who also has revisional jurisdiction: incidentally, he receives a large share of the fines imposed by the caste councils.

Religious leaders have also great influence in Mysore, where it is enhanced by organization, for they have numerous agents who submit reports to them and transmit their orders to the castes, more especially the Brahmans and Lingayats. In the south of the Bombay Presidency the spiritual heads of different communities decide all important caste cases, and it is said that several caste councils have almost been relegated to the position of inquiring and reporting agencies under them.

Mention should be made in this connexion of the part which is played by the Guru, who in some sects need not be a Brahman. A Guru is the spiritual preceptor of a number of families, whom he visits in turn, and in North India corresponds to a family priest or father-confessor. In South India he is more. There, as Dr Francis Buchanan (afterwards Buchanan-Hamilton) wrote:

> In their judicial capacity the Gurus possess great authority. They take cognizance of all omissions of ceremonies and actions that are contrary to the rules of cast (*sic*). Small delinquencies they punish by pouring cow-dung and water on the head of the guilty person, by fine, and by whipping. For great offences they excommunicate the culprit. The excommunication may be removed by the Guru, in which case he purifies the repentant sinner by a copious draught of cow's urine.[1]

Landlords also sometimes intervene in purely caste matters on their own estates, more particularly in Bengal, Orissa and the north of the Madras Presidency. Their intervention may be sought by the castes themselves, if the landlords are men of old family and high character, who command their respect. Such a landlord is in the position of an arbitrator, to whom even Brahmans refer disputes. In other cases aggressive and not too scrupulous landlords have encroached on the liberty of the castes, and have done so deliberately in order to coerce their tenants and keep them under their thumb. They appoint headmen, decide on caste questions themselves, and pocket the fines which they impose, as well as fees for marriages and other ceremonies.

[1] *A Journey from Madras through the countries of Mysore, Canara and Malabar* (1807), vol. II, pp. 146–7.

Chapter IV

PENALTIES

EXPULSION from a caste involves penalties, both temporal and spiritual, similar to those which attended, or were believed to attend, excommunication from the Christian Church. A man who was excommunicated was cut off from intercourse with other members of the Church. None might eat or speak with him, none receive him in distress. If he remained under the ban of the Church and was not readmitted to Christian fellowship, he died without sacraments, he was refused the rites of Christian burial, and he was believed to be doomed to eternal damnation. So too the Hindu who is outcasted is as one cut off from among his people. He is debarred from intercourse or association with his caste fellows, none of whom will eat, drink, or smoke with him. His own kindred disown him; he cannot get his children married; he is deprived of spiritual ministrations, for Brahmans will not perform religious or domestic ceremonies for him. Other castes cooperate in enforcing the ban which is laid upon him, and he is unable to obtain the services which ensure personal cleanliness, for washermen will not clean his clothes, and barbers will not shave him or cut his hair. And if he is still an outcaste when he dies, his funeral will take place without the rites which will ensure his salvation hereafter: without them a man is doomed to misery as a disembodied evil spirit. Social excommunication, in short, involves religious disabilities in this life and spiritual damnation hereafter.

It is matter for small wonder that the prospect of such a punishment with its present fears and horrible imaginings prevents transgressions of caste ordinances. Sir Walter Lawrence gives a telling instance of its deterrent effects. A Hindu friend of his had twice paid a visit to England, and had twice been readmitted to caste fellowship after paying a heavy fine. He was warned, however, that if he made the voyage a third time he would not be let off so lightly. He was asked by Government to go again to England, and Sir Walter Lawrence urged him to do so in disregard of caste scruples. He replied, "Would you defy caste if you knew that you and those dear to you would be outcasts and, when they die, dragged by scavengers to the burning *ghāt*?" As Sir Walter Lawrence himself justly observes: "The threat of 'sixty thousand years in hell' appals the bravest".[1]

Permanent expulsion from caste is a punishment reserved for the most heinous offences,

[1] *The India we served* (1928), p. 165.

including conversion to Christianity or Islam. For other offences a man is put out of caste temporarily, often with the idea of allowing him a *locus poenitentiae* and in the hope that the suspension of social intercourse may effect a reformation. A man may be outcasted either for a definite period or until he performs a ceremony of purification called *prayaschitta*, after which caste fellowship is resumed.

A common form of expiation is tasting a mixture of the five products of the cow (*panchgavya*), viz. cow-dung, cow's urine, milk, curds and clarified butter (*ghī*), which is a sovereign purge for impurity. A modern substitute for this nauseous mixture is *panchāmrita*, i.e. a nectar of five substances, viz. milk, curds, unclarified butter, honey and sugar; the last two, it will be noticed, take the place of cow-dung and urine. *Panchāmrita* is said to be as efficacious as *panchgavya* for minor offences, but the latter is necessary for major offences, especially a voyage to Europe. That continent is held to be a land of the Mlechhas or barbarians, residence in which was forbidden to the twice-born in the Laws of Manu. There is a growing tendency to indulgence towards those who have broken this ancient rule. In orthodox circles a mild expiation, such as tonsure of the head and a payment of money to Brahmans, is sometimes allowed; unorthodox circles dispense with any expiation.

Even in Nepal, where hitherto the State had insisted on an expiatory ceremony, the rule was relaxed for soldiers who had served outside India during the Great War. They received a general indulgence provided that they had neither consciously broken the caste law nor stayed away longer than was actually necessary.

Among the lower castes the readmission of outcastes is very often celebrated by means of a common feast. The fact that the caste men publicly eat and drink with them testifies to their restoration to caste privileges. The original sentence of temporary excommunication is not always carried out. It may be commuted to a fine, or a repentant sinner may have the ban raised simply by showing signs of contrition and removing the cause of the offence. One such case was that of a carpenter who became drunk and abused the members of the caste council. For this unseemly conduct he was outcasted for six months, but the sentence was remitted as soon as he apologized. A barber, who was outcasted for twenty-five years because he had shaved men who were the regular customers of another barber, escaped this heavy sentence at the price of paying for a feast to all the barbers living in the neighbourhood.

Restoration to caste is not always as simple as this. The communal feast may be preceded by elaborate purifications. Among the Uralis in

Trichinopoly if a man has seduced a girl of the caste, the two have to be married and are purified together with their relatives. First they have to bathe in 108 different pools of water. Then they have to walk over a plot of ground in which the head of a sheep has been buried and have their foreheads smeared with its blood. This is followed by more bathing. Next they drink cow's urine and bathe again. And then at last they give the caste council a feast.[1]

It is curious to note that some castes recognize, either explicitly or implicitly, a scapegoat or sin-eater when expiatory ceremonies are performed. Among the Uppiliyans of Trichinopoly a ceremony of purification for caste offences is performed by a man designated "the man of two lights", who is given a meal to eat in the polluted house with his hands tied behind his back.[2] In the Central Provinces several castes pay a man called the *agua*, or leader, to eat the first morsel of food at a penitentiary feast and so take on him the sin of others.

Owing largely to the absence of a regular system of trials, excommunication, either temporary or permanent, is the general form of punishment in force among the higher castes. If a man is suspected of an offence, his castemen cut off intercourse with him, and he remains out

[1] *Trichinopoly District Gazetteer*, p. 113.
[2] *Ibid.* p. 117.

of communion until he proves his innocence or expiates his offence. If he does neither, he remains, and will die, an outcaste. Among the low castes, on the other hand, there is an extraordinary variety of penalties both in kind and degree. An offence which in one place involves expulsion from caste will in another be let off with a fine. An endeavour is made in many cases to make the punishment fit the crime. Penances of a religious nature are prescribed for personal pollution and for various religious or semi-religious offences, like sacrilegious acts, the omission to perform due ceremonies, etc. They include bathing in the Ganges (in places where it is near) and swallowing some of its sand, immersion in cold water—the head as well as the body should be submerged—drinking water in which a Brahman has dipped his toe, a pilgrimage to a holy place, tonsure of the head, and the feeding or giving of presents to family priests and Brahmans.

Some of the penances imposed for causing the death of a cow by neglect or carelessness, and not of malice prepense, e.g. if it is strangled in its stall by the rope round its neck, or is accidentally drowned in a pond, have a symbolical character. The culprit has to beg for his food for a certain length of time, which may extend to years, and must not speak but may make inarticulate sounds like the lowing of a cow.

Sometimes he is accompanied by a cow whose tail he holds or he carries a staff on which the tail of the dead animal is tied. Or the owner may be required to pay the price of several cows, and if he has not got the money, must beg from door to door till he raises it, with a rope round his neck and some straw in his mouth; according to one account, he should wear the hide of the dead cow complete with horns and hoofs.

For non-religious offences fines are commonly imposed. A cash payment may be required, or the council may order the payment of the cost of a common feast, or the contribution of food, utensils, or articles used at such feasts or at meetings of the caste council, like pots, pitchers, and matting. The fines are graduated according to means and are often petty.

Only the low castes resort to corporal punishment, and even among them it is becoming rare, partly because of the fear of criminal proceedings being instituted by a man who has been chastised, and partly because it is not considered dignified and respectable by castes which are endeavouring to improve their social position. Such castes have taken to consulting Brahmans and substituting the expiatory ceremonies recommended by them for this shorter and more summary procedure. The tradition of its value, however, lingers: by immemorial custom one caste always has bamboo twigs ready for use at council meetings, though they are rarely brought into action. When corporal punishment is inflicted, it takes the form of a thrashing with bamboos, sticks or shoes: the use of shoes adds insult to injury. Among the low-caste Purbias of the Punjab a delinquent who pleads inability to pay is actually kicked out of the council meeting by four of its members and is outcasted till he finds the money. An unusual form of corporal punishment is that of a prolonged cold bath, which is in vogue among the Nats in North Bihar. A man may be required to sit in cold water for a period varying from two to twenty-four hours according to the season and the gravity of his offence. A case is known of a man who sat in the water of a river for some hours on a cold winter's day and was then induced to come out by a kind-hearted passer-by, who saw him shivering with cold. Unfortunately the period of the sentence had not expired; and his disobedience being an aggravation of his original offence, he was outcasted for five years.

What is far more common is the imposition of some punishment of a humiliating nature. This takes many forms, which show considerable ingenuity on the part of their inventors. Shoes are often brought into action, e.g. a man may be compelled to wear a string of old shoes round his neck, or to collect the shoes of his caste fellows and carry them on his head. Shaving of the head or moustaches, or both, is also resorted to: in part of the Central Provinces a favourite punishment for an illicit intrigue is to shave the head and moustaches of the man, and to cut off a lock of his paramour's hair, besides requiring them to provide a feast. Ridicule is added by shaving one part of the head or one side of the moustaches, and further ignominy by a public parade of the victim. A common traditional punishment inflicted in some localities consists of making a culprit ride on a donkey with one half of his face coated with lime, and the other half smeared with tar. A milder punishment is to make a man stand for a certain length of time in the sun with a pitcher full of water poised on his head—to make him stand on one leg is an additional refinement—or he may have the heavy mortar which is used for pounding rice hung from his neck. Women may be punished for loss of virtue by having to walk round the village with a grinding stone round their necks.

Contemptuous penalties are also in vogue: wealthy men, who can afford to pay heavy fines, are in this way sentenced to pay insignificant sums equal to a penny or two or a fraction of a penny. This is a subtle form of humiliation which is keenly felt by those subjected to it, who would far rather pay fines proportionate to their means. One curious punishment of this nature is found in Orissa. There a man who has been fined, but is too poor to pay the fine, is ordered, in default, to prostrate himself before an assembly of his caste people and to present each with the twig which serves Indians for a tooth-brush, together with some water.

Equally, if not more, extraordinary are the punishments of this kind imposed by some of the castes in Madras. Among the Valaiyans unchaste women have to carry a basket of mud round the village, and men who are habitual offenders against morality are forced to sit on the ground with their toes tied to their necks. Among the Ravulos a husband who ill-treats or deserts his wife has a prolonged humiliation to endure. First of all, he has to go inside a large fish-trap (like a hen-coop in shape) and his wife sits on it. Both then go to the part of the house in which corpses are washed and are treated like corpses, i.e. pots of water are poured over them. The wife then acts as if she were actually a widow, i.e. she smashes a cooking pot and breaks her bangles. This having been done, she returns to her father's house and is free to marry again. In Cochin a Nambudri Brahman woman who is guilty of adultery is not only outcasted, but funeral ceremonies are performed for her as if she was dead. In parts of the Punjab a Chamar who has abducted a married woman has to suck her breasts as a sign that he regards her as his mother and then restore her to her husband on pain of excommunication.[1]

Punishments are varied according to the popular estimate of the enormity or triviality of an offence and the motives and means of the accused. There is generally an honest attempt to do justice; a distinction is made between voluntary and involuntary offences; extenuating circumstances are taken into consideration; and punishments are graduated. On the other hand, the system is open to the grave objection that it admits of vicarious punishment and neglects the principle *Non reus nisi mens sit rea*. Men and women are often punished for results for which they are not personally responsible or in any way to blame. Many instances might be given of the way in which guiltless members of a family suffer for the malfeasance of one of their relations, but one will suffice. In Bengal, if a wife who has eloped is taken back by her husband, not only may he be outcasted but also his family; if an unchaste widow is given shelter in her parental home, her father may be outcasted.[2]

Purification is necessary for purely accidental contact with those whose touch defiles, and men may be outcasted for having taken food or drink with men of whose low caste, and consequent

[1] *Punjab Census Report for 1911*, Part I, p. 424.

[2] See R. C. Dutt, *The Peasantry of Bengal* (1874), p. 71.

polluting qualities, they were in ignorance. Again, if a man of a respectable caste has a quarrel with one of a lower caste and has the misfortune to be so much the weaker that the latter beats him with his shoes, he must be purified. In the Central Provinces this is a simple enough matter. It is merely necessary to take a bath or to drink water which has been sanctified by a Brahman dipping his toe in it; and it is not even necessary to do this if the assailant is in the privileged position of a policeman or a Government peon (*chaprāsi*).

The most poignant case in modern times of innocent suffering is that of many thousands of Hindus who were outcasted *en masse* because they had been forcibly converted to Islam during the Moplah rebellion in Malabar in 1921. Compulsory circumcision, which is an effective means of conversion, was only one of the accompaniments of brutal and unrestrained barbarism, such as massacres, outrages upon women, pillage and arson, which were perpetrated by the Moplahs until troops were hurried up to restore order;[1] but the fact that they were innocent victims could not save their caste. They remained out of communion until they had undergone the ceremony of *panchgavya* (i.e. tasting the nauseous mixture of five products of the cow already mentioned), and had

[1] *India in 1922–23* (Calcutta, 1923), p. 264.

paid Brahmans the fees demanded for performing that ceremony.

Even more pitiable was the fate which used to be reserved in Bengal for those wretched persons who, having been taken to the Ganges to die, had the ill fortune to recover. It should be explained that the river Ganges is revered as a goddess (under the name of Ganga) and that the same sanctity attaches to any of the ancient channels, like the river Hooghly, by which it has found its way to the sea. Hindus along its banks take out their relations, when apparently on the point of death, to die in its holy water. The dying man (or woman) is immersed to the waist and mud from the sacred river is put into his mouth, for one of the ancient Hindu scriptures (the *Agni Purānā*) sets forth that those who die when half their body is immersed in the water of the Ganges will be in bliss for thousands and thousands of ages. Those seemingly moribund persons who survive are regarded as having been rejected by the goddess Ganga, and they used to be rejected also by their families and castes and forced to live apart. This custom, now happily extinct, was the basis of Rudyard Kipling's *The Strange Ride of Morrowbie Jukes*, a gruesome story of "the Dead who did not die but may not live", who were consigned to a pit in the desert, Rudyard Kipling remarking *passim* that a somewhat similar institution used to flourish on the outskirts of Calcutta.

Accounts written about a century ago are eloquent upon what non-Hindus would consider the inhumanity of this treatment. One states:

> When a person has been taken to the side of the Ganges, or other substituted waters, under the supposition that he is dying, he is, in the eye of the Hindoo law, dead; his property passes to his heir; and, in the event of recovery, the poor fellow becomes an outcast. Even his own children will not eat with him, nor afford him the least accommodation; if, by chance, they come in contact, ablution must follow. The wretched survivor from that time is held in abhorrence, and has no other resort but to associate himself in a village inhabited by persons under similar circumstances.[1]

There were in fact two villages inhabited by these innocent outcastes. The one was Sukhsagar, which Lady Nugent, wife of the Commander-in-Chief in India, described in 1813 as a village "inhabited by the poor wretches who have recovered after being exposed by their relations to die on the banks of the river. They lose all their claims on society, their caste is gone for ever, and no one can associate with them without incurring the same penalties. They therefore

[1] Loc. cit. J. Peggs, *India's Cries to Humanity* (1832), p. 172.

have formed a little colony here of themselves".[1] The other village was Chakdah, now a small town in the district of Nadia. We are told:

When any of the unfortunate individuals who are carried to the river survive...they are generally expelled from their cast (*sic*), torn from their relations, and sent to inhabit this village [Chakdah]. There they intermarry, and I suppose live as comfortably as any of the low cast Hindoos.[2]

Even as late as 1887 Mr Wilkins wrote:

A large village near Calcutta is occupied by the descendants of these outcastes, who have intermarried with each other, unmindful of their former caste distinctions because they were now equally regarded as outcastes. But this practice has now ceased, the few who survive being permitted to rejoin their families.[3]

The survival of persons who have been taken to the banks of the Ganges to die is still regarded as disgraceful, though they are no longer excommunicated. Mr S. C. Bose, himself a Hindu, writes:

In the case of an old man the return home after immersion is infamously scandalous; but in that of an aged

[1] Lady Nugent, *A Journal from the year 1811 till the year 1815* (1839), vol. II, pp. 197–8.

[2] Loc. cit. J. Peggs, *India's Cries to Humanity* (1832), p. 187.

[3] W. J. Wilkins, *Modern Hinduism* (1887), p. 451.

widow the disgrace is more poignant than death itself. I have known of an instance in which an old widow was brought back after fifteen immersions, but being overpowered by a sense of shame, she drowned herself in the river after having lived a disgraceful life for more than a year.[1]

In conclusion, it should be stated that, though outcasting involves social and religious disabilities, it does not involve any loss of civil rights in British India, for the Caste Disabilities Removal Act of 1850 expressly declared that any law or usage which inflicted forfeiture of rights or property, or which might be held to impose or affect any right of inheritance, by reason of anyone being deprived of caste should no longer be enforceable in the courts of law.

[1] *The Hindus as they are* (Calcutta, 1883), p. 258.

Chapter V

MARRIAGE AND MORALS

IT has been said that caste is mainly a matter relating to marriage, and it is certainly true that there is nothing to which the caste pays such attention as the maintenance of its marriage customs. Whatever else may be neglected, the strict observance of its marriage law is insisted on. If there is even a whisper of suspicion of a breach of it, the caste moves at once: it is quick to suspect and prompt to punish. The object is to preserve the purity of the stock and even more, perhaps, the chastity of the women belonging to the caste. Whether or no the general custom of early marriage among Hindus is due to the desire to ensure the virginity of brides, the result of that custom seems to be that a high standard of feminine virtue is exacted and practised, as is also the case among the Irish peasantry. Among the latter, as Lecky has pointed out in his *History of European Morals*, the habit of marrying at the first development of the passions has produced an extremely strong feeling of the iniquity of irregular sexual indulgence.

The nearly universal custom of early marriages among the Irish peasantry has alone rendered possible that high standard of female chastity, that intense and jealous sensitiveness respecting female honour, for which, among many failings and some vices, the Irish poor have long been pre-eminent in Europe.

The marriage customs of the castes vary so greatly as almost to defy general treatment. Endogamy, exogamy and hypergamy are all in force, and to give a full account of the system, if it can be called a system, it would be necessary to string together an immense number of peculiar and uncorrelated facts. Briefly, however, it may be said that in all cases there can be no marriage within the prohibited degrees, and that where, as is generally the case, a caste is endogamous, the bride and bridegroom must be of the same caste and also of the same sub-caste. If a caste (like the Rajputs) is exogamous, the parties must be of the same caste but must belong to different septs or clans: each clan depends on other clans for its wives. Where again hypergamy is practised, men of a higher sub-caste or sept can take wives from a lower, but women must marry into one of the same or a higher status.

Apart from these rules, the marriage system has certain features, of which the first and foremost is the universality of marriage and the second the early age at which it is generally celebrated. It is necessary for every Hindu to marry so as to have a son, for his salvation after death depends on offerings duly made by one lawfully begotten: if a man has not got one, he should adopt a son, who will be as capable of performing the necessary rites. It is further believed to be necessary for an orthodox Hindu to get his daughters married before the age of puberty:[1] an unmarried daughter is a matter for reproach and causes a family to be looked down upon. The essential thing is that the marriage ceremony should be performed: after it is over, the girl remains in her father's home and does not go to her husband's to live with him until she attains puberty. So essential is the marriage ceremony that it is performed *pro forma* in some strange fashions. In some parts, if a husband cannot be obtained for a girl before puberty, she goes through a form of marriage to an arrow, a flower or a tree. A marriage ceremony is recognized as a necessary rite even for a girl who is intended for prostitution—the negation of marriage: she is married to a knife, or a sword, or a plant, or to a man, generally an imbecile, who is only a *pro forma* husband. If an adult Nambudri Brahman girl dies unwed, the family honour is saved by paying a man to go through a form of marriage with the corpse.[2]

For some time past the age of marriage has

[1] The Child Marriage Restraint Act of 1929 (popularly called the Sarda Act) has made marriages of boys under eighteen and of girls under fourteen illegal, but this has not prevented such marriages.

[2] *Madras Census Report for 1901*, Part 1, p. 56.

been gradually rising among the higher castes partly because of education and enlightenment and partly because of economic considerations. Parents arrange for their children's marriages—it is not a matter of free choice—and a daughter's marriage is an expensive necessity for a man of high caste. Large amounts have to be paid to the bridegroom's father, and the marriage itself, with its attendant festivities and entertainments, is a costly affair. Many are, therefore, obliged to wait till they have saved enough to meet the expense involved. There are also some exceptions to the general rule about early marriage. Adult marriage is common both among the Nepalese and in castes of aboriginal descent, which have the sensible belief that a wife should be old enough, and strong enough, to do house and other work.

Marriage is a sacrament[1] which, according to orthodox Hindu belief, a woman can perform only once in her life, and consequently the marriage of widows is strictly prohibited by respectable castes. It makes no difference whether a woman is a widow who has lived with her husband or is a technical widow, a virgin for whom the marriage ceremony has been performed. The marriage of widows is permitted by many low castes, but the parties frequently have to obtain

[1] Among the Nairs and other castes of the west coast of Madras it is not a sacrament nor indissoluble, but is revocable at the will of either party.

the sanction of the caste council, which gives its consent only after it has considered the propriety or advisability of the marriage. When the marriage takes place, the ceremony is conducted with maimed rites: there may even be nothing more than the presentation to the bride of some clothes and ornaments including bangles. In Orissa a widower may marry a widow in most castes; if a bachelor intends to do so, he is first married to a tree, which is cut down so as to make him symbolically a widower. The low castes tend to give up widow marriage in imitation of the high castes. Its abandonment is regarded as a hall-mark of respectability, for the castes which forbid widow marriage rank higher than those which allow it; even in the same caste a sub-caste which discontinues it claims on that account a status higher than the sub-castes whose widows contract second marriages.

The levirate is found among low castes and aboriginals, i.e. the custom by which a widow marries a brother of her deceased husband. It differs in several respects from the levirate of the Jews described in Deuteronomy, for the widow need not be a childless widow, she can marry only a younger (and not an elder) brother of her late husband, there seems to be no idea of "raising seed unto a brother", and the marriage is not obligatory, as among the Jews, but optional. Either party may refuse to contract the union, but it is regarded as the proper thing for the woman to marry again in this way, and the caste people will try to persuade her, if she is reluctant, though they will not force the marriage on her.

Divorce is also opposed to the sacramental idea of marriage,[1] but is also permitted by many low castes, on such grounds as the unchastity of a wife or her failure to bear her husband sons. Even among them, however, it is regarded as a concession to a husband rather than as a right. The consent of the caste council has usually to be obtained, and this operates for the protection of a wife, for the caste council will not allow divorce to be undertaken lightly or unadvisedly. A divorced wife is debarred from remarrying except among the lowest castes.

Although chastity is demanded from women, strict continence is not expected from men. Concubinage is almost a popular institution in Orissa. There it has long been the custom, when a marriage takes place in the families of Rajas and wealthy landlords, for the father-in-law to provide the bridegroom with a number—it may be as high as fifty or more—of young unmarried

[1] A Bill to allow Hindu wives to divorce insane, leprous, or impotent husbands, which was recently introduced in the Indian Legislative Assembly, was hotly opposed on religious grounds, its opponents expressing abhorrence to its provisions.

girls as maidservants. The recipients of these wedding presents act on Horace's advice *Ne sit ancillae tibi amor pudori*: and the girls have a recognized place in the household. This curious practice is being given up, but concubinage is met with among members of the higher castes who can afford it. It is subject to the provision that the concubines must belong to clean castes. It has actually given rise to a distinct caste, the Shagirdpeshas (meaning servants), which is some 50,000 strong. It consists of the offspring of such irregular unions and their descendants, and the fissiparous tendency of caste is shown by its being divided, according to the caste of the father (Brahman, Khandait, Karan, etc.), into separate sub-castes, between which there is no intermarriage.

Little or no discredit attaches to men having mistresses, provided that they belong to castes from which they may take water and that they do not eat food prepared by their paramours or feed with them. If these conditions are observed, the caste takes no notice of the intrigue. If they are not, the caste may outcaste the man. Liaisons with women of unclean castes used to be punished in a draconian way. A Nambudri Brahman of Malabar who had a liaison with a Shanan woman (who is an "untouchable") was blinded, and so was his paramour, while her relations were either put to death or sold as slaves to the Moplahs, Moslems by religion, who exported them overseas.[1]

Adultery is even now sometimes punished by death though, being murder under the criminal law, all knowledge of it is usually suppressed. As a case in point may be mentioned the terrible results of the liaison of a Goala in Bihar with a married woman, who was his cousin. He escaped with his life but was outcasted. The woman was burnt to death with her husband, the latter presumably sharing her fate because he connived at the adultery. By ancient custom a Nepalese husband had a right to slay a man who had an adulterous connexion with his wife. The right was subject to two restrictions. The adulterer, who was unarmed, was given a start of a few yards, but this rarely saved him from being cut down by the outraged husband, as he was usually tripped up by the latter's friends. He could also save his life by passing under the husband's uplifted leg, but this was considered such an outrage on honour that few would save their life by taking advantage of it. The exercise of the husband's right of vengeance unto death continued until comparatively recent times, but has become practically obsolete. A man is allowed to put it into practice only after the

[1] See F. Buchanan, *A Journey from Madras through the countries of Mysore, Canara and Malabar* (1807), vol. II, pp. 416–17.

matter has been submitted to the Prime Minister and all attempts at compromise have failed.[1] The husband is now usually awarded by a court of law or arbitration the amount of his marriage expenses, which the adulterer has to pay. The latter, if too poor to pay, occasionally claims the right to compound by undergoing the dishonour of passing under the husband's leg.[2]

The castes exercise the keenest vigilance in regard to the marriage law and a scandal is soon detected. Relations are broken off with the erring parties, and also often with their families. Such action is taken by tacit and common consent among castes which have no governing bodies. Those which have them bring the matter up before the caste councils, which act as tribunals for trial and punishment. Few of the cases with which they deal are thought so serious or are so severely punished as breaches of the marriage law, such as marriage outside the caste or sub-caste, adultery and seduction.

The caste councils and caste headmen also do a lot of miscellaneous and useful work in settling matrimonial disputes, in deciding questions of maintenance, in seeing to the restoration of runaway wives, and enforcing the performance of marriage contracts and the payment of the sums

[1] P. Landon, *Nepal* (1928), vol. 1, p. 175.

[2] See W. Brook Northey and C. J. Morris, *The Gurkhas* (1928), pp. 102–3.

promised to a bride's father in the case of low castes. The "price"[1] to be paid for a bride (or for a bridegroom in the case of high castes) is generally settled by mutual agreement among the parents, but in some cases it is settled by the caste council. Some castes also control their members so far as to pass sumptuary laws regarding the maximum expenses to be incurred on marriage ceremonies; and they may even prescribe the ages at which marriages may be contracted. The Namasudras in Bengal some years ago resolved at a general conference that anyone who married a son under twenty or a daughter under ten years of age should be put out of caste; and in one locality it was laid down that if a father was rich, he should take no bride price for his daughter, and if poor, not more than Rs. 30, a sum then equal to £2.

Reference may fittingly be made here to the salutary reforms effected among the Rajputs and other castes in Rajputana on the initiative of Colonel Walter, Agent to the Governor-General in Rajputana. Anxious in the interests of the Rajputs themselves to reduce the ruinously heavy expenses of their marriages, and to prevent child marriages, he persuaded the Rajput chiefs to agree to a reformed system and in 1888 founded an association to carry it into effect.

[1] The "price" is a marriage fee paid to parents, and there is no actual purchase.

This body fixed the maximum proportion of a man's income which might be devoted to the expenses of a marriage, and it prescribed eighteen as the minimum age at which a boy might be married and fourteen for a girl. It has also laid down that no girl should remain unmarried after the age of twenty, and has prohibited second marriages during the lifetime of the first wife, unless she is childless or suffering from an incurable disease. Monogamy is almost universal among Hindus and the taking of a second wife, though not positively forbidden, is regarded by the upper classes as dishonourable except for these two causes or failure to bear a son after a long period of years.

The influence of the caste councils extends beyond questions of marriage and is exercised in a healthy manner in keeping up the moral tone of the community, in maintaining a standard of decency and propriety, and in promoting peace and good-will among its members. A council, and also a headman, acts as a general *censor morum*. Disputes about inheritance are decided by them; family quarrels are amicably settled and reconciliations effected; abuse and assaults by one man on another are punished; nor are the spreading of false rumours and disrespect to elders too small for their notice.

Castes are jealous of their good name and fame unless they are criminal castes, i.e. castes whose hereditary occupation is some form of crime and whose greatest pride is a successful theft or burglary. With these may be contrasted a caste in Madras mentioned by Dr Francis Buchanan, the Gollaru or Gollanwallu, who cultivated the land and acted as a village watch-and-ward.

> This caste has, besides, a particular duty, the transporting of money both belonging to the public and to individuals. It is said that they may be safely entrusted with any sum...and they consider themselves bound in honour to die in defence of their trust....They have hereditary chiefs called Gotugaru who, with the usual council, settle all disputes and punish all transgressors against the rules of caste. The most flagrant is the embezzlement of money entrusted to their care. On this crime being proved against any of the caste, the Gotagaru applies to the Amildar or civil magistrate, and having obtained his leave immediately causes the delinquent to be shot.[1]

To come to modern times, it is interesting to notice the way in which castes with any pretensions to respectability will deal with black sheep who are a disgrace to them. The Malis of Sambalpur in Orissa call on a man who has been sent to prison by a court of law more than once to execute a bond undertaking not to commit crime on pain of expulsion from caste; and a man who

[1] *A Journey from Madras through the countries of Mysore, Canara and Malabar* (1807), vol. 1, pp. 347–8.

is imprisoned seven times is outcasted for ever. Other castes in Orissa outcaste a released convict until he has been on a pilgrimage and provided a caste feast; but this is probably due to the pollution caused by his not having been able to observe the caste rules about food and drink while in jail. In the Central Provinces similar considerations affect the attitude of the castes to those who have been in prison. A man is outcasted if he has had to eat food prepared by a man of another caste, but not if he has been a civil prisoner and so able to prepare his own; he is also generally outcasted if he has had handcuffs put on him.

From time to time low castes, which have a deservedly bad reputation for theft and dishonesty, by common consent resolve to reform. In the early years of this century the Dosadhs in one district of Bihar resolved at a mass meeting to break off social relations with any who were habitual thieves and who were convicted in the criminal courts, and no longer to marry, eat or drink with any Dosadhs who received them in communion. They followed this up by handing over to the police some notorious criminals. The movement died down after a time, and the caste relapsed into dishonesty; but seven years later there was a revival, as a result of which the crime in one area was reduced by half. On this occasion the Dosadhs approached the head of the local police on their own initiative and promised to deal with any dishonest member without criminal proceedings. In 1921 again a very low caste of untouchables in the same neighbourhood, the Doms, passed a similar ordinance, resolving to have no social relations with anyone who persisted in criminal courses.

Chapter VI

FOOD AND DRINK

THE orthodox Hindu regards the eating of certain kinds of food as something more than the means of obtaining sustenance or of satisfying the appetite. A meal is not merely, as in Europe, a domestic or social function, but almost a sacrament to be celebrated with due ritual. It is hedged round by restrictions as to the way in which it should be prepared and the company in which it should be eaten. These restrictions, however, apply only to the food called *kachchi*, i.e. food cooked with water, such as boiled rice and pulses and wheaten cakes, which constitute the main part of the daily diet of an Indian. If it is cooked away from the family kitchen, elaborate precautions are taken to ensure its purity. A space is marked off and plastered with mud, or preferably cow-dung, if it can be got, for cow-dung has great purifying virtue. Into this space outsiders may not pass; untouchables, like Europeans and Hindu low castes, may not cast their shadows on it: if such an untoward thing happens, the food is defiled and must be thrown away. The Raj Gonds, a Hinduized section of the Gonds, with the perfervid zeal of new converts, outdo even Brahmans in ceremonial nicety, for they wash the wood which is used for cooking; but this is a work of supererogation.

Before eating, an orthodox Hindu should wash his hands and feet. He sits down stripped to the waist except for the sacred thread; and he can eat with no one who is not a member of his own endogamous circle, i.e. caste and sub-caste. Shylock's remark might well have come from a Hindu: "I will buy with you, sell with you, talk with you, walk with you, and so following; but I will not eat with you".

One exception is made to the rule of exclusiveness. All pilgrims to the shrine of Jagannath at Puri, whatever their caste, may eat together of the food called *mahāprashād*, i.e. food which has been sanctified by presentation to the god. All men are equal in the sacrament of this holy food, and it is popularly believed that if a man of low caste offers it to one of higher caste, and the latter turns his head away in scorn or by way of refusal, his neck will remain rigid in that position. This is very possibly a survival from the times of Buddhism, which repudiated caste distinctions. The doctrine of equality in the sight of the god is qualified to some extent in actual practice, for a certain number of untouchable castes are refused admission to the temple and have to be satisfied with making their offerings to an image at the entrance gate.

If a man away from home cannot prepare his own *kachchi* food, it must be prepared by a man of his own caste and sub-caste unless he employs a Brahman as a cook. Many castes do this because the fact that a Brahman will serve them is a patent of respectability. Brahmans are also employed as cooks in jails, so that caste susceptibilities may not be offended. For Brahmans themselves the question of a cook is more complicated. Sir William Hunter saw a Brahman convict in Bengal try to starve himself to death and undergo a flogging rather than eat food cooked by a fellow Brahman from the north-west of India, because of scruples as to whether the cook's birthplace was equal in sanctity to his own.[1] Mr Alan Butterworth mentions the case of a Brahman of North India living in a Madras district who was reduced to extreme straits by similar sensitiveness. He drew a mere pittance of a pension with which he could get enough food to feed his children but not himself, and he was emaciated by hunger. The Madrasi Brahmans, touched by compassion and fellow-feeling for a Brahman, would readily have given him food, but he would not touch it. Mr Butterworth came to the rescue with money, to the acceptance of which there was no objection, and the Brahman was enabled to buy food for himself. "There is", as Mr Butterworth says,

[1] *Indian Empire* (1892), p. 242.

"more than a little fineness in that preference of lingering misery on earth to the risk of a spiritual stain."[1]

Neither a Brahman or other orthodox Hindu of any but the very lowest caste would accept food from either a European or a Moslem. Cases have occurred before now of Hindus whose lives were saved by Europeans giving them food but who lost their caste in consequence, even though they were unconscious when food was administered to them. They lived to curse their would-be benefactors, whom they regarded as their worst enemies, and, incidentally, expected to be maintained by them for the rest of their lives.

The punctilious exclusiveness which the high castes observe in regard to *kachchi* food is proverbial among the Indians themselves. One proverb runs, "Thirteen Rajputs, thirteen cooking places"; another, less literal and more satirical, says "Three Tirhut Brahmans and thirteen cooking places". The proverbs are not so exaggerated as might be thought. Any college with resident students has to employ a plethora of cooks owing to their different castes. At the University College at Lahore there were a hundred cooks who went out on strike a few years ago rather than cook for a student of low caste; and Mr W. E. S. Holland has told us

[1] *The Southlands of Siva* (1923), p. 164.

that when he was in charge of a hostel at Allahabad he had to provide thirty-seven kitchens for a hundred students.[1] Mr E. C. Candler wrote from personal observation of Brahman sepoys on active service during the Great War:

> I remember watching a class regiment in the Essin position; their habit of segregation had spread them over a wide area. Each man had ruled out his own pitch; and a Turk would have taken the battalion for a brigade. Only in the case of near relatives will two men sit in the same *chauka*. In spite of the cold, one or two of them were naked except for the loin cloth. The others wore vests of wool, which (apart from the loin cloth) is the one and only material that Brahmans may wear at meals. All had first bathed and changed their *dhoti* according to the prescribed rites, and carried water with them to wash off any impurity from their feet when they entered the *chauka*.[2]

Fortunately for the convenience of Hindus when away from their homes, there is another kind of food which can be eaten fairly freely. This is food which has been cooked with *ghī* or clarified butter, such as concoctions of flour, vegetables, and the sugary confections and sweetmeats which the people of India love, and which they can buy at confectioners' shops.

[1] *The Indian Outlook* (1926), p. 26.

[2] *The Sepoy* (1919), pp. 129–30. The *chauka* is the "pitch" marked off for cooking and eating; a *dhoti* is a loin cloth hanging down to the knees.

There is much to be said for Mr W. Crooke's remark that "Hinduism is elastic enough to ignore its own rules when they are practically unworkable, and provides one class of food for the traveller and another for the man living at home".[1]

Food of this kind, which is called *pakki*, may be eaten without preliminary bathing, without removing the clothes, and in company with persons belonging to other castes. It can be eaten by the twice-born castes after it has been handled by men of those Sudra castes which are regarded as clean, of whom the confectioners are one. Those castes are known generically as *Navasākhas*, a Sanskrit name meaning the nine branches. In point of fact they are not limited to this number, and different castes are held to be clean in different parts of the country.

The orthodox explanation is that *pakki* food is purified by being cooked with a product of the sacred cow, viz. *ghī*. This (unless adulterated) is considered so pure that it cannot be contaminated or made unfit for use by the touch of even the lowest castes.[2] This explanation, however, does not take into account the fact that *pakki* food is not confined to articles cooked with *ghī*, but includes other articles like parched rice

[1] *Things Indian* (1906), p. 229.

[2] J. N. Bhattacharya, *Hindu Castes and Sects* (Calcutta, 1906), p. 262.

and fruit, and that there are no scruples as to the popular stimulant called *pān-supāri*, which every one buys and chews without bothering about the castes of those who have handled it.[1]

In southern and western India the higher castes will, as a rule, take water only from persons of their caste and sub-caste, but in northern India they are not so exclusive, for Brahmans and other twice-born castes will drink water that has been fetched or touched by men of any clean Sudra caste. They can also take Ganges water (but not any other kind of water) from men of unclean castes. Ganges water is of such transcendent purity that it cannot be contaminated even by untouchables. In practice no one drinks out of a vessel belonging to anyone of another caste. It would be legitimate to do so if the owner of the vessel belonged to a higher caste, but the latter would not allow it as his vessel would be defiled by the lips of a man of lower caste. There is not the same objection however

[1] *Pān* is the aromatic leaf of the betel plant (*Piper betel*), which forms the outer cover of this dainty. The inside of the leaf is smeared with slaked lime mixed with catechu, and on it are placed areca nut (*supāri*) and various spices. The leaf is then folded over and made into a small triangular packet, which is put whole into the mouth and chewed. It is almost part of the daily diet: every one who can afford them chews several packets a day and some chew dozens of them. It is regularly presented to those who attend the ceremonial receptions called Durbars, at which no one minds its being handed round on trays by an Englishman.

to a man drinking water poured into his cupped hands from another man's vessel, which in this way is kept free from taint. All will take water from Brahmans, who are consequently employed to supply water to thirsty railway passengers by pouring it into their cupped hands, cups or other vessels.

There is a saying *Apah pavan shuddhanti*, i.e. "water is purified by air", which is explained as meaning that water poured out by unclean hands is made pure by aeration. This is quoted to justify the practice by which some Hindu families in Delhi have water poured into their household vessels from the leather water-bags of Moslem water-carriers. This is most exceptional, for nothing is so polluting as leather: if he has touched anything made of leather, a Hindu should not merely wash his hands, but scour them with earth, before touching food or drink. But there is a parallel, for in the west of the Punjab the combined effect of Moslem influence and scarcity of water is that Hindus use water-bags made of leather for holding water.[1]

Nothing is so essential to the preservation of caste as pure water, and men have died before now rather than take it from a man whose touch pollutes. St James's Church in Delhi was built by Col. James Skinner in fulfilment of a vow which he made while lying wounded on a

[1] *Punjab Census Report for 1911*, Part 1, p. 411.

battle-field. He had been left there for dead and lay for two nights and a day suffering agonies from thirst and the pain of his wound. Near him lay a Rajput officer who had lost a leg. A Chamar, who is an untouchable, came along with water, which Skinner drank; but the Rajput refused, saying that he would rather die than be defiled; and he consequently died.

It is largely on account of the difficulties in connexion with water that sea voyages cause pollution and loss of caste until the pollution is purged by the performance of purifying rites, for nowhere is it so hard to obtain a sufficient stock of water that is free from all taint to a Hindu as on board ship. The difficulty may be got over by taking a supply of Ganges water, and this is sometimes done, but not every one can bear the expense. Recently accounts have appeared in the newspapers of a Brahman delegate to the Round Table Conference having brought to England large casks of water from the Ganges and having arranged for a weekly supply to be sent from India. There are also difficulties with regard to food, besides which the twice-born are forbidden by the Laws of Manu to reside in any land of the Mlechhas, or barbarians, of which Europe is held to be one. Expiations may therefore be required from those who have travelled overseas either because they have disobeyed this injunction by going to a

Mlechha country or simply because they have broken the law of purity in the matter of food, water and ceremonies. The Nepalese envoys who used to go to China with tribute had to undergo a rite of purification on their return to their own country, even though they went overland and did not cross the sea.

The *raison d'être* of the interdict on sea voyages is not known to the unlearned masses. They see the effect and are ignorant of the cause. They merely know that a sea voyage involves loss of caste; the *kālā pāni*, as the sea is called, is consequently full of horror to them. This was the plain unequivocal attitude of a regiment of the Bengal army which mutinied in 1824 during the first Burmese war because of an unfounded rumour that it was not to march to Burma overland but be transported there by sea. "They could," they declared in a written memorial, "never put foot on board ship, and none would forfeit his caste. For this reason all had sworn by Ganges water and the *tulsi* plant that they would never put foot on a ship." Later, some of the regiments of the Bengal army were recruited on the express condition that they would not serve overseas, but this proved such a source of practical inconvenience that, in 1856, a general order was issued by Lord Canning that in future no one would be recruited who would not agree to serve wherever he might be required. This was one of the grievances of the army before the Mutiny of 1857.

That Mutiny, as is well known, was occasioned by the sepoys having to use cartridges with greased papers, the ends of which had to be bitten off before loading the new Enfield rifle. The grease was composed of beef fat, to which the Hindus objected, or of lard, to which both they and the Moslems objected. It will be noticed that there was no question of eating anything, merely of contact with the lips and teeth. So, too, in earlier days Hindus lost caste if beef was placed in their mouth without their consuming it. This was a device of Moslems anxious to force Hindus to adopt Islam, as they might be expected to do in desperation at the loss of caste.

Pollution therefore can be caused merely by forbidden things coming into contact with the mouth. For this reason Hindus will not lick postage stamps if they can help it, because of suspicions about the purity of the gum, but moisten them with water; and they will on no account use European tooth-brushes made of pig's bristles. The continued use by Europeans of tooth-brushes which have been defiled by saliva is looked upon as horrible. For the same reason smoking in company is subject to the same rule as the eating of *kachchi* food, i.e. a man can only smoke with his castemen, because the pipe is a hookah or hubble-bubble which passes not merely from hand to hand but from mouth to mouth, each man applying his lips to it and inhaling the smoke. In northern India a common expression for outcasting a man is *hukkā pāni band karnā*, i.e. to cut off smoking and drinking with him.

In this connexion the common mode of eating of the Hindu may be noticed. He rolls up his rice into a ball of convenient size and, holding his head back, pops it into his open mouth without his hand touching the latter. Similarly it is quite common to smoke a cigarette without putting it between the lips. It is held in the fingers and the hand is curved round to form a funnel, through which the smoke is inhaled: contact of the mouth with gummed paper is thus avoided. This and other practices already alluded to undoubtedly have their origin in hygienic considerations: Pandit Harikishan Kaul, indeed, says, "Pollution according to the Hindus is caused physically by the contact of sputum and by transmission of bacteria by touch or even by the breath".[1]

Hindus are not only subject to inhibitions in regard to the persons by whom their food may be cooked, those from whose hands it may be taken, and those in whose company it may be eaten; they are also governed by unwritten laws

[1] *Punjab Census Report for 1911*, Part I, p. 411.

and traditions as to the kinds of food which may properly be eaten. Some birds and animals are too sacred to be killed or eaten. Because of their sacred character peacocks are carefully preserved in Hindu States; even outside them there has been many a fracas between Hindu villagers and sportsmen ignorant of the veneration in which peacocks are held, but in some parts there is no objection to shooting them. As for beef, eating it is as much a sacrilege to the orthodox Hindu as the desecration of the Host would be to a Catholic. One of the Ministers of the Maharaja of Kashmir and Jammu (in whose territory, a man could at that time be imprisoned for life for killing an ox) told Sir Monier Monier-Williams that if he had to choose between being beheaded and being forced to eat beef, he would unhesitatingly prefer death by decapitation.[1] This point of view is typical and not exceptional. There is the same objection to killing oxen, and in some States the slaughter of cattle is absolutely prohibited in consideration of the susceptibilities of the Hindu population. Even those untouchables who will eat beef will not kill an ox or a cow, but merely eat the meat of those which have died a natural death.

1 *Modern India and the Indians* (1878), p. 234. The slaughter of a cow in Kashmir is still a penal offence but the maximum penalty is only seven years' imprisonment: the law on the subject is not a dead letter but is enforced.

Other kinds of food are too vile to be eaten, as, for example, the flesh of that foul feeder, the domestic pig: there is not the same prejudice to the flesh of wild pig, which is greatly relished by Rajputs. Other foods are tabooed for various reasons. The Laws of Manu forbade the twice-born to eat domestic fowls, onions and garlic, turnips and carrots, salted pork and mushrooms. Some castes of aboriginal descent have objections based on totemism, e.g. to mutton; other castes abhor lentils and tomatoes because their colour resembles blood.

It is extremely hard to generalize as to what is permissible or not, as practice varies so greatly. Much depends on locality and on the abundance and cheapness of different articles of food. Fish is almost universally eaten in Bengal and also in some districts of Assam, where it is abundant; in Bombay some Brahmans along the coast eat it fried; other Brahmans, such as the Chitpavan Brahmans of Bombay, will have none of it. Much also depends on the extent to which Brahmanical influences have impressed themselves on the mass of the people. The words of St Peter, "I have never eaten anything that is common or unclean", express the standard which the orthodox Brahman sets for himself and for others. In particular, he abstains from spirits and animal food, but he has been unable to bring the low castes up to his standard. In this, as in other respects, Hinduism is not synonymous with Brahmanism, and practice does not conform with Brahmanical precepts. The low castes are, as a matter of fact, mainly vegetarians, but it is from necessity rather than choice. Most of them will eat meat, such as mutton and goat's flesh, if they can get it, but they can rarely afford it. A proverb current in South Bihar expresses the view of these unregenerate Hindus, viz. "A meal of fowl, fish, and meat, with vegetables well pounded, preceded by *ghī* (clarified butter) and finishing with curds—that is rightly called a meal". Nowhere is there such freedom as in Nepal. The Nepalese will eat meat of any kind except the flesh of cows and female goats and (in the case of Brahmans, Chettris and Ghales) fowls. Pork is not objected to: the marriage ceremonies of the Rais are said to conclude with the parents of the bride and bridegroom exchanging presents of "the inevitable leg of pork and jar of spirits".[1]

Much again depends on whether a religious sect prohibits a particular diet. In North India Vaishnavas are strict vegetarians, and Kabir-panthis abjure both meat and intoxicating liquor, but Saivas, of high as well as low castes, will eat mutton and goat's flesh. The question of meat-eating is often a thorny one. The Arya

[1] See W. Brook Northey and C. J. Morris, *The Gurkhas* (1928), pp. 94, 244, 259.

Samaj[1] was split by schism over it in 1893, one section, called the Mahatma party, objecting to it, the other, called the College party, being in favour of it. A sub-caste of the Vellalans, who rank next to the Brahmans in Madras, is divided into two sections composed of meat-eaters and vegetarians, which will neither intermarry nor eat together. So strong is the feeling on the subject that the vegetarian section will not admit into its ranks any one who has had a meat-eating ancestor up to the two-hundred and third generation.

In no respect has the strictness of the caste system been so much modified as in the matter of food and drink. The spread of education and western ideas among the higher classes has led to increasing laxity, at any rate in the towns and away from their homes. In the villages the force of public Hindu opinion is strong, and the conservative influence of the women of the family is a formidable obstacle even to advanced thinkers. In the towns there is more liberty of thought and action; educated men of different castes will eat and drink together at private parties and will not scruple to eat forbidden food at hotels and restaurants. The lower classes also have been affected by the spread of railway facilities and the industrial development of the country. Caste restrictions are neglected by

[1] This is a sect, founded about 1875, which has its greatest strength in the United Provinces. It has a monotheistic creed and advocates social reforms, such as raising the age of marriage, allowing widow marriage and relaxing caste restrictions.

passengers crowded together in a railway carriage, and they are apt to go to the wall under the conditions of factory life.

The Brahmans have found it difficult to apply their rules to new foods and drinks, and modern science has often defeated ancient prejudice. As a rule they have adapted themselves to new conditions—a triumph of expediency over orthodoxy. The cultivation of the potato was introduced into Bengal by the English in the latter half of the eighteenth century, and for a long time its consumption was banned by orthodox Brahmans, but now all who can afford potatoes and like to eat them do so without scruple. Few again have any scruples about taking tea or products of applied science, such as biscuits, soda water and artificial ice.

The Brahmans have shown a certain subtlety in adapting their views to the general convenience and justifying themselves on religious grounds. Medicines compounded by Europeans were once considered impure—it was (and still is) a common belief that spirits are among their ingredients—but a Sanskrit text was unearthed to the effect that a physician is like the god Narayan, who removes pain, and medicine is as the water of the Ganges; on the strength of this the ban was lifted. The prejudice against European medicines has not altogether disappeared; it is expressed by Mr Gandhi, who in *Hind Swaraj* or *Indian Home Rule* wrote:

"Doctors violate our religious instinct. Most of their medical preparations contain either animal fat or spirituous liquors". Another pious fiction came into use when a modern water supply was introduced in Calcutta. The difficulty was that the water was drawn from taps on hydrants in the streets, to which every one, Moslem and Hindu, low caste and high caste, had access. It was first suggested that separate taps should be made available for high caste Hindus, and when this was ruled out, the situation was met by the ingenious theory that the water-rate which had to be paid was a penance which expiated the use of the taps.

A contrast to this accommodating attitude was presented by the firm stand which the Brahmans in Calcutta made in 1917 when the purity of a product of the cow, viz. *ghī* (or clarified butter) was in question. *Ghī* is used not only for the preparation of food but also for religious ceremonies and offerings. Trouble arose from the fact that it was being adulterated on a large scale with cheap animal fats. Its purifying virtue was consequently lost and the ceremonies and offerings were vitiated. Large profits were being made from the sale of the adulterated article by the Marwaris, astute merchants well known for their attachment both to Hinduism and to money-making. The Brahmans called on the Marwari Association to excommunicate those who were carrying on the trade in adulterated *ghī*, and when it was slow to respond, took action themselves. They directed that those of their number who had used the impure product should undergo a ceremony of purification on the bank of the river Hooghly, which, as an old channel of the Ganges, shares in its sanctity. Thousands of Brahmans gathered there, lit fires of purification, which were fed with *ghī*, and fasted for some days, chanting sacred verses called *mantras*. The Marwari Association was galvanized into action and appointed a Panchayat. Three committees dealt with the cases of the three castes concerned, Agarwalas, Masheshwaris and Brahmans. After a sitting lasting nine hours it was decided to excommunicate two Brahmans for two years and three months respectively, in addition to fines, and to excommunicate for one year the heads of two Agarwala firms, besides fining one of them a lakh of rupees (then equivalent to £6666) and the other a quarter of that sum. The Brahmans were satisfied and the ceremony of purification was brought to an end. The Association next moved the Bengal Government to introduce legislation penalizing the manufacture and sale of adulterated *ghī*. The Governor, Lord Ronaldshay (now the Marquess of Zetland),[1] acted with great promptitude, and within three days a Bill was passed into law.

[1] Lord Ronaldshay gave a vivid account of the whole affair in *India: A Bird's-eye View* (1924), pp. 209–11.

Chapter VII

OCCUPATIONS

THERE is a common idea that every caste has a hereditary or traditional occupation which all its members must follow. This idea has led to statements to the effect that if one knows a man's caste, one can tell his occupation. This, however, is a fallacy. It is true that many castes, in particular functional castes, have a hereditary calling, and that, in some cases, many of their members follow it; but there is no actual obligation to do so, except perhaps among some criminal castes which seem to regard a life of crime almost as a positive duty. Of a few occupations it may be said that they are either so high or so low that only certain castes engage in them. The priestly avocation is one, washing clothes is another. In North India, if a Hindu is found working either as a priest or a washerman, it would be safe to deduce that he is a Brahman or Dhobi, in the one case because only Brahmans can exercise sacerdotal functions, and in the other because washing is such a vile and degrading occupation that it is left to the Dhobis whose traditional occupation it is. On the contrary it would be quite unsafe to deduce from the fact that a man is either a Brahman or a Dhobi that he earns a living as a priest or a washerman. Caste, in short, cannot be regarded as a certain clue to occupation.

Even the Laws of Manu, though inculcating that each of the orders should follow its own calling, allowed considerable latitude in case of necessity. If a Brahman could not subsist by teaching the Vedas, he might earn a livelihood as a soldier. Should he fail to get a subsistence by that, he might take up the occupations of Vaisyas, i.e. commerce, or agriculture, or the keeping of cattle; and a Kshattriya, if driven by distress to give up his true calling, i.e. the pursuit of arms, might do the same; but neither a Brahman nor a Kshattriya might till the soil himself. Similarly, Vaisyas were permitted to adopt lower occupations in order to support themselves, and Sudras, unable to maintain their families by service to the twice-born, might subsist by handicrafts.[7]

Throughout the ages Brahmans have not been confined to their proper avocation of studying and expounding the Hindu scriptures but have adopted secular professions. Government and administration have especially been Brahmanical professions. Under Hindu rule the king's ministers and councillors were mainly Brahmans, and they have not forgotten their former political power. The memory of it is still green, and has not a little to do with their struggle to maintain their ascendancy under a semi-democratic system.

To come to later times, the Maratha armies in the eighteenth century were largely officered by Brahmans.

> "It is remarkable", wrote Sir Alfred Lyall, "that in the warlike Maratha federation, which subsisted by violent inroads and plundering, the paramount power had by the eighteenth century fallen into the hands of a Brahman family. Not only was the Brahman Peshwa a military chief who commanded troops in person, but his Maratha army was mainly officered by Brahmans; and as the western Brahmans are by custom and profession remarkable rather for intellectual and literary capacity than for physical energy or hardihood, the conversion of them into soldiers shows how far the military spirit of the times had prevailed over sacerdotal or Levitic tradition.[1]

Brahmans formed a strong element in the army of the East India Company, and at the time of the Mutiny the sepoys were popularly known by the name of one branch of Brahmans[2]. They were called Pandies, which is a corruption of *Pānde*, the title of a branch from which many

[1] *Asiatic Studies* (1884), pp. 291–2.

[2] According to a contemporary estimate, a regiment 1000 strong would as a rule contain about 200 Moslems and 800 Hindus, viz. 200 Brahmans, 200 Rajputs and 400 men of lower castes. *The Mutiny of the Bengal Army* (*The Red Pamphlet*) (1857), p. 6.

men in the ranks were drawn: the first man shot for mutiny was one Mangal Pande. After the Mutiny Brahmans continued to be recruited for the Indian army, though in diminished numbers, and the Brahman connexion with the army was till recently maintained in one regiment.[1]

The majority of Brahmans are now engaged in secular pursuits: special statistics compiled in Bengal during the census of 1921 showed that only one-fifth followed their traditional occupation. They are found in the public services and the police, in trade and in the learned professions; they have been described as "*par excellence* the schoolmasters of the country".[2] Many are land-holders, both great and small, and large numbers are in domestic service. So many work as cooks that Jogendra Nath Bhattacharya has remarked that the name of Thakur, which is an honorific designation of Brahmans, has suffered a strange degradation, for though it means "god", it is now very often taken to denote a cook.[3]

[1] The 4th Battalion of the 1st Punjab Regiment (formerly called the 1st Brahman Infantry and, later, the 1st Brahmans), which was disbanded in 1932, was composed of Garhwali Brahmans and Punjabi Musalmans. The 10th Battalion of the same regiment contains Garhwali Brahmans besides other classes.

[2] Sir Bampfylde Fuller, *The Empire of India* (1913), p. 131.

[3] *Hindu Castes and Sects* (Calcutta, 1896), p. 22. Thakur is more familiar to the English public in the form of Tagore owing to the literary fame of Rabindra Nath Tagore.

There are two main reasons for the abandonment of hereditary occupations, one economic and the other social. The first is connected with economic developments, which may make it impossible for a caste to continue to carry on a particular industry or trade. The number which can be employed in or supported by any industry depends on the demand for its products. India has now come within the ambit of world-wide trade, and its old village handicrafts are giving way before machinery and the mass productions of modern mills and factories. Weavers, to mention a typical case, have found the fabrics of their hand-looms driven out of the market by imported piece-goods, and weaver castes have had to give up weaving and earn their daily bread by labour and other means. Again, in any particular locality, a functional caste may increase so largely in numbers that the demand for its products is insufficient for the support of all its members; and there is no alternative left but for some of them to change to some other means of subsistence. Factors such as these prevent the activities of a caste being restricted to its hereditary avocation.

The second reason is the ambition of the low castes to raise themselves in social esteem by adopting some pursuit which by common repute is more respectable than their ancestral calling. There is a particular tendency to change handiwork for trade. Handicraftsmen and artisans first become middlemen of their own products and then blossom out as general dealers. A fisherman who has saved some money sets up as a fishmonger, and next drops the sale of fish and takes up the sale of other articles. Or a clean sweep may be made and an entirely new means of livelihood adopted, such as agriculture. These changes lead to fission in the castes themselves. It is common for a section which has adopted a more reputable calling to break off relations with those who still cling to the traditional vocation, to arrogate a higher social status, and to develop into a new sub-caste or, occasionally, to form a new caste.

Social ambition of this kind is laudable enough: it is based on a certain sense of self-respect: but unfortunately it does not remove or mitigate the stigma of birth in places where, and so long as, the origin of the men in question is known. A potter, a fisherman, a barber or a worker in leather may be a cultivator—and cultivation is an honourable estate—but they remain as unclean in general estimation as their unregenerate brethren who still make pots, catch fish, etc.

A change of occupation is not objectionable *per se*. What is objectionable is the adoption of a means of livelihood which is regarded by the caste itself as degrading. This may be illustrated by the case of the Brahman. Certain occupations involve a loss of prestige; others are considered so disreputable as to cause actual degradation. Brahmans who serve as the priests of idols in temples are considered to have a low status without, however, losing their Brahmanhood. Those, however, who either officiate at the cremation of corpses (which involves pollution by proximity to dead bodies) or serve unclean castes as priests, are not recognized as Brahmans by members of their caste. They retain the name of Brahmans but not the reverence paid to Brahmans. The touch of the Mahabrahmans, who are in the former class, is polluting to an orthodox Hindu—the name means great Brahman and is derisory and contemptuous. The Barua or Vyasokta Brahmans in Bengal, who are in the latter class, are in such low esteem that even those castes whom they serve will not eat food in their houses.

Brahmans are also debarred from tilling the soil, or to use the Indian phrase, touching the plough. They may engage in agriculture, but must be like gentlemen farmers, employing labourers for manual work. The Rajputs share this aversion from the plough, and in the Kangra Hills relegate to a lower grade any man who so far debases himself as to plough.

At meetings of the tribe and at marriages the Rajputs undefiled by the plough will refuse to sit at meals with the plough-driver, as he is contemptuously called, and many, to avoid the indignity of exclusion, never appear at public assemblies. The probable reason is that the legitimate weapon of the Kshattriya or military class is the sword; the plough is the insignia of a lower walk of life, and the exchange of a noble for a ruder profession is tantamount to a renunciation of the privileges of caste.[1]

The low castes have no objection to ploughing but have their own category of despised occupations, the adoption of which may render a man liable to expulsion from his caste. One of them held in special contempt is the manufacture and sale of intoxicating liquor; in Madras the Shanans and Iluvans, who perform these useful functions, can cause pollution to a Brahman if they come within twelve yards of him. No work, however, is more abhorred than that connected with dead bodies, human and animal, or with hides and leather; the Doms who perform menial work connected with the last offices to the dead are among the lowest of the low. The dread of losing caste on account of anatomical work was long an obstacle to surgical science. Medical students would not dissect corpses but learnt anatomy by means of models made of wax or wood. The name of the first Bengali, Madhusudan Gupta, who nearly a century ago had the courage to break with tradition and engage

[1] Sir Denzil Ibbetson, *Panjab Castes* (Lahore, 1916), p. 156.

in dissection when the Medical College in Calcutta was opened, is still held in remembrance and honour there. Equal heroism was shown by that very gallant gentleman, Sir Partab Singh of Jodhpur, who, after tending a young English officer during his last illness, insisted on being one of those who carried him to his grave, scouting the warnings of the Brahmans that he would lose caste.[1]

The making and selling of shoes are nearly as bad as skinning an animal and dressing the hide. Leather in any form has peculiarly polluting qualities: the proverb, "There is nothing like leather", holds good in India but has implications very different from those given to it in England. During the first Afghan war the rigours of the climate compelled the Brahman sepoys to wear sheepskin jackets, with the result that when they returned to India

> they were regarded with horror by their brother soldiers and co-religionists; among civilians as men without caste—worse spiritually and temporally than if they had never known caste—men who had refused to perish rather than violate their religion; and the people considered them like certain apostates described in the New Testament, "twice dead, plucked up by the roots".[2]

[1] See Sir Walter Lawrence, *The India we served* (1928), p. 206, and J. Buchan, *Lord Minto* (1924), p. 232.

[2] E. H. Nolan, *History of the British Empire in India and the East*, p. 341.

How strong the prejudice can be in a conservative community may be realized from an amusing story told by Mr Tyndale Biscoe in *Kashmir in Sunlight and Shade* about the first game of football played in Kashmir in 1891. He had great difficulty in introducing the game simply because a football is made of leather, but succeeded in getting a game started. It was suddenly stopped, amid general consternation, because the ball had hit a Brahman boy in the face. The boy lifted up his voice and wept at the idea of defilement; but the ready wit of Mr Tyndale Biscoe saved the situation. He had the boy taken off to the canal to purify himself by bathing; the players trooped off with him, and when a bathe had restored the boy to purity, the game was resumed. So completely has this prejudice died down that football is now extremely popular in India.

This is a small, but significant, instance of the change of feeling among the educated classes in the towns. The higher castes there have largely emancipated themselves, not only from such prejudices, but also from the former restrictions on their means of living. Brahmans and other high castes have taken an active part in starting and managing tanneries and leather factories, wine shops, and other businesses which by custom and tradition are debarred to them.

When there is an hereditary occupation, a

certain number of the caste follow it as a matter of course. This is more especially the case in the villages, which, it should be remembered, contain nine-tenths of the population of India. The villages have been for centuries largely self-contained and self-supporting, though their isolation is giving way before the extension of roads, railways, the motor-bus, etc. Certain handicraftsmen, such as potters, blacksmiths, barbers and washermen, have always been recognized members of the village community as well as inheritors of a caste calling, and are known generically as village servants. To a large extent they still have assignments of land in return for their services, and in many areas are paid in kind, and not in cash, receiving shares of the actual produce of the village crops.

It is a normal thing for one son at least in a family belonging to a functional caste to succeed to his father's craft, provided that it suffices for a living and provided also that he has not been educated for a higher calling. So far from deploring the system, some satisfaction may be derived from the fact that a boy is born into the world with an inalienable right to follow a particular calling, and that it is a father's duty to train him in his own craft. The result is an inherited skill exercised generally with the simplest of tools.

In some ways the organization of the functional castes resembles that of the medieval guilds. Those guilds were corporations which issued regulations prescribing *inter alia* the hours of work and providing against unfair competition. The warden of the guild and a certain number of guild brethren formed a court which enforced its ordinances. Disobedience to their orders was punished by fine or, in the last resort by expulsion, and a wrong done by one guild brother to another was treated as a wrong against the general body of the guild and visited with similar punishments. A common fund was raised by contributions and was utilized for religious offerings as well as for promoting the common interests of the guilds.

A caste is not a guild, for members of the latter had no community of blood and membership ceased on abandoning the trade or industry common to the guild, whereas a caste is connected by intermarriage and membership of it is retained when an occupation is given up. Functional castes, however, have many points of resemblance with the guild. It is a primary rule among them that one man must not take away another's customers. So strong is the proprietary sense that recognized rights to work for certain families are sometimes sold, like a goodwill, mortgaged, and given in dowry. An encroachment on another man's rights is severely dealt with, even to outcasting in some places, though in others, e.g. in the Punjab, the offender may be merely fined. One barber was outcasted for working for a man who had been the customer of a fellow-barber, even though the latter had been dismissed by him; in a similar case the penalty was excommunication for twenty-five years, though this was afterwards commuted to the provision of a feast for the caste brethren. The despised castes whose members work as scavengers and sweepers are particularly strict in maintaining established rights and, in doing so, often tyrannize over their employers. A quarrel with the necessary menial who does the dirty work of the house, removes night soil, etc. frequently puts a private householder in a quandary as no other sweeper will agree to work for him. There is a similar difficulty when municipal scavengers go on strike. The conservancy work is at a standstill till the scavengers come to terms or, as sometimes happens, a new staff of scavengers of a different caste is imported.

Like the guild, the functional caste has a common council which makes regulations besides punishing the breach of them. The caste council may order a general strike and outcaste a blackleg. It fixes trade holidays: a criminal case once came before me in which the Kaseras or braziers of a town had ordered the last day of the month to be observed as a holiday, and they expelled from the caste a man who tried to steal a march on the others by working on that day. The Sonars or goldsmiths in one district of the Central Provinces have an annual meeting, with a common feast, at which they take an oath that no one will, on pain of being outcasted, reveal the trade secret of the amount of alloy which is to be mixed with the precious metal. Lastly, the functional castes, like the guilds, have common funds which are expended, as stated in Chapter II, on common caste purposes.

In Bombay and Baroda there are some true guilds, consisting of men of different castes, which co-exist with, and sometimes dominate, the industrial and trading castes. They punish offences against their regulations and customs, e.g. working overtime, accepting low wages, and acting as a blackleg by taking up work thrown up by another man who has had a dispute with his employer. In the city of Baroda there is a general guild, called the Mahajan, with jurisdiction in trade matters over the whole town. This body has a very effective organization and exercises a full measure of control over all the trading communities. Only the Baniya or trading castes and the higher castes are represented on the Mahajan, but all the trade guilds are subordinate to it. It fixes rates of wages, the hours of working, and the holidays to be observed; it directs when there shall be strikes or a general closure of the shops and, on the other hand, when there shall be a general feast. It intervenes even in social matters, such as marriages and divorces, and to some extent overrides the caste councils of the trading classes: anyone dissatisfied with an order of the latter may appeal to the Mahajan, and its decision is law to the caste council. The tendency is, however, for it to confine its authority to matters of trade and to leave social questions alone.[1]

[1] *Baroda Census Report for 1911*, Part 1, p. 252.

Chapter VIII

THE UNTOUCHABLES

UNTOUCHABLE is a name of comparatively recent origin applied generically to persons in the lowest classes of Hindu society. It implies that they cannot be touched by orthodox Hindus of higher caste without consequent contamination; but the idea among Hindus themselves is that the untouchables cannot touch others without making them impure: the position, in the words of a Hindu writer, is that "their touch means contamination, water touched by them is polluted". They are also commonly referred to as "the depressed classes", and are sometimes called "the outcastes" or "the outcaste Hindus" as distinguished from higher castes, which are referred to as "caste Hindus".

The term outcastes is, however, a misnomer, for the untouchables have castes just as much as other Hindus. They have their own gradations of caste and their own standards of caste honour, which they are punctilious in maintaining. An untouchable can himself be polluted by the touch of another untouchable belonging to a lower caste and may be outcasted if he takes food from him. A century ago James Forbes wrote of two untouchable castes in Malabar:

> The Pooleahs are not permitted to breathe the same air with the other castes nor to travel on the public road; if by accident they should be there and perceive a Brahmin or Nair at a distance, they must instantly make a loud howling, to warn him from approaching until they have retired or climbed up the nearest tree.... Yet debased and oppressed as the Pooleahs are, there exists a caste, called Pariars, still more abject and wretched. If a Pooleah by an accident touches a Pariar, he must perform a variety of ceremonies and go through many ablutions before he can be cleansed from the impurity.[1]

The Pooleahs (who are also called the Cherumans) are thePulayans, a name meaning "those who cause pollution." They themselves, if polluted by the near approach of a Nayadi or Ulladan, have to take seven baths and shed a few drops of blood from the little finger. The Pariars are the Paraiyans (Pariahs), of whom Bishop Caldwell gave a description which is equally applicable to other untouchable castes. They "constitute a well-defined, distinct, ancient caste", with "subdivisions of its own, its own peculiar usages, its own traditions, and its own jealousy of the encroachments of the castes which are above it and below it. They are,

[1] *Oriental Memoirs* (1834), vol. 1, pp. 253–4.

equally with the higher castes, filled with that compound of pride of birth, exclusiveness and jealousy called 'caste feeling' ".[1]

Various estimates have been made of the number of those who come within the category of untouchables. The figure has been put as high as sixty millions and as low as thirty millions, the variations depending on the tests adopted, but the latest estimate is 43,600,000 persons, which was made by the Simon Commission on the criterion of causing pollution by touch or by approach within a certain distance. This total represents nearly 30 per cent. of the Hindu population.[2]

This social residuum is heterogeneous in character. It includes castes of aboriginal extraction, castes which have low or degrading occupations, and a number of other castes working as artisans, cultivators and field labourers, whose occupations cannot be called unclean. It is not difficult to understand why some castes should be held in contempt. Their manner of life, their promiscuous food, their intemperate habits and drunkenness, render them repulsive to abstemious and clean-living Hindus. For example, the Musahars of South Bihar, who for centuries have been little better than serfs, live in filthy

[1] *Comparative Grammar of the Dravidian or South Indian Family of Languages* (1875), pp. 545, 546.

[2] *Report of the Simon Commission* (1930), vol. I, p. 40.

hovels and feed on rats, mice and snails, in addition to coarse grain: the very name means rat-eater or rat-catcher. Mr R. C. Dutt voiced the views of the general Hindu community when he wrote:

> In every village in Bengal where semi-aboriginals live, a separate portion of the village is reserved for them, and the most careless observer will be struck with the difference between neatness and tidiness, the well-swept, well-washed and well-thatched huts of the Hindu neighbourhood, and the miserable, dirty, ill-thatched huts of the Bauri *pārā* or the Hari *pārā*.[1] If a cow or a pig dies in the village, it is flayed, and the meat carried home by the Muchis or Bauris, while the Hindus turn aside their face and stop their nose in disgust when passing near such scenes. If there is an outstill in the village, it is in the Bagdi *pārā* or in the Bauri *pārā*; it is thronged by people of these castes, who spend their miserable earnings here, regardless of their ill-thatched huts and their ill-fed children.[2]

There is no such justification for the ignominious treatment meted out to others, who are in no way inferior, whether in manner of life or means of livelihood, to many of those by whom they are scorned. They are in good company (though that is no consolation to them), for in the estimation of orthodox Hindus Englishmen

[1] *Pārā* means a hamlet.

[2] "The Aboriginal Element in the Population of Bengal", *Calcutta Review*, 1882.

and Europeans are equally untouchable. British residents in India are not always aware that some of the Hindu gentlemen with whom they shake hands think it incumbent to remove the consequent contamination by bathing. This is one of the reasons why orthodox Hindu gentlemen like to call on British civil officers early in the morning before the time at which they take their bath.

In South India the idea of untouchability has been carried to an absurd length. Contact with some castes causes pollution, but others are worse, for their mere presence or proximity defiles higher castes: it is a case of unapproachability rather than untouchability. There is even a scale of distances within which different Panchamas, as the untouchables are called in South India, may not approach Brahmans, e.g. eight yards for Kammalans, twelve yards for Iluvans or Tiyans, sixteen yards for Pulayans, thirty-two yards for the Paraiyans or Pariahs. In rural areas in Travancore, Cochin and Malabar, a Pariah may be required to keep further away and is prevented, at any rate in the day-time, from using the roads in quarters inhabited by Brahmans. His right of way along other roads is so far limited that, like a leper in the medieval ages in Europe, he should call out to give notice of his unclean presence, and when he comes within the prescribed distance, leave the road and get along, as best he can, in the fields, even if they are under water. The time required to go from one place to another consequently depends, not merely on distance, but on the number of Brahmans using the road. Unapproachability of this kind is almost unknown elsewhere. It is becoming less common in the places where it exists, and the bathing required to remove pollution is not infrequently omitted except by the most orthodox.

The galling wounds to self-respect and the actual inconvenience caused by such a belief can easily be imagined. Boys may take hours going a comparatively short distance to school, because of the number of Brahmans to be avoided on the way; very possibly they would not mind this if it were not that they are punished for being late. Again, in some areas a Panchama making a purchase from a shopkeeper has to go through a long and humiliating process. He places money on the ground in front of the shop and withdraws to a safe distance. The shopkeeper then comes out with the goods, puts them on the ground, and takes up the money. The Panchama finally advances after the shopkeeper is back in his shop and removes his purchases. Many similar stories could be told of the absurd results of the system in South India, such as that of a co-operative society whose members included Brahmans, clean castes and untouchables, and sat at different levels at meetings so as not to breathe the same air and cause atmospheric pollution.

In North India generally there is no idea that the untouchables have, as it were, an emanation of impurity extending to a certain distance. There untouchability is a matter only of actual contact. It means that orthodox Hindus of higher caste cannot take food or water from one of them, that it is thought necessary to bathe after contact with them, and that they are debarred from using the same wells and bathing places and sometimes also the schools: an untouchable boy may either be kept out of the village school, or be made to sit separately in a class, or in the verandah outside the school rooms. There is no objection to their using the roads like anyone else, and in some parts common sense prevails so far that only a few unclean castes, like scavengers, leather-dressers and shoemakers, rank as untouchable. Elsewhere, however, as in Bengal, an orthodox Hindu of high caste will not even enter the house of a liquor manufacturer, if he can help it, and if obliged to do so, will change his clothes and bathe himself.

The religious disabilities of the untouchables are generally much the same, e.g. as regards entry into temples. This does not prevent their making offerings to the gods. They bring their little offerings of fruit, flowers and confectionery, which they make over to a temple priest, and wait outside the shrine till he comes out again and, after returning the baskets or trays in which they brought the offerings, dismisses them with his blessing. It should be pointed out in this connexion that Hindu worship is not congregational and that the worshippers, even if they belong to clean castes and are able to enter the temples, do not make offerings personally. A Hindu temple is not intended for a congregation, but is a shrine for the idol and for the performance of ceremonies by priests, and offerings are made, not by the votaries themselves but by priests acting on their behalf.

Social disabilities vary from province to province and even in different parts of the same province. Practice varies more especially in the cities and the villages. The rule about bathing if one has come into contact with an untouchable is generally adhered to in the villages. In the cities, where it may be necessary to bathe a dozen times a day if one is puritanical, the formality is commonly dispensed with. On the other hand, the belief in untouchability still has such force that if a stranger lies ill or dying in the streets, orthodox Hindus will not move a finger to help him for fear that he may be an untouchable.

The idea of untouchability appears to be least prevalent in the Punjab and Assam.

According to a statement prepared by the Punjab Government for the Simon Commission, some 2,268,000 persons in the Punjab might technically be regarded as belonging to untouchable castes; but untouchability is merely held to mean that food touched by them cannot be eaten by high caste Hindus; it is only in the case of actual scavengers that bodily contact involves pollution.[1] Access to the richer Hindu temples is debarred to all persons included in the figure given above, but minor temples are not closed to them; and in other respects there is a great variation in the degree of liberty given in social intercourse. The problem of the untouchables in the Punjab is, in fact, said to be like that of other classes which are socially and economically backward; and there is scarcely a problem at all in Assam, where there is little difference between them and non-Hindu aboriginals.[2]

To illustrate the general position of the untouchables I may be permitted to reproduce an account which I gave of the Gandas of Sambalpur (in Orissa) in the Census Report of Bengal, Bihar and Orissa, and Sikkim for 1911.

[1] In the *Punjab Census Report for 1911* it was stated: "Till recently a sweeper walking through the streets of the larger towns was supposed to carry a broom in his hand or under his arm-pit as a mark of his being a scavenger and was expected to shout out '*Bacho, Bacho*' (Look out) with a view to preventing people from being polluted."

[2] *Simon Commission Report* (1930), vol. 1, pp. 39, 67.

They are so degraded that a twice-born Hindu considers it necessary to bathe if he is touched by one of them; formerly a Brahman was defiled by a Ganda even casting his shadow over him. They are not allowed to draw water from the village tank, the village barber will not shave them, the village washerman will not wash their clothes. No orthodox Hindu rides in a cart if a Ganda happens to drive it, wears a garment if a Ganda has stitched it, sits on a floor if a Ganda has plastered it, drinks wine if a Ganda has distilled it, or purchases vegetables if a Ganda sells them. A Ganda in suffering receives no sympathy and the door of Hindu charity is ordinarily closed against him. Until recently, moreover, no Ganda child was allowed to join the village school, and though they are now allowed to attend it, they must sit apart from other Hindu boys. They cannot enter a Hindu temple, take part in Hindu religious ceremonies, or even build their houses in the village with other Hindus.

In spite of all this, the lot of the untouchables is not as hard as might appear at first sight. They have the fellowship and friendship of men of their own caste, they have their own festivities as well as the fun of the local fairs. Deprivation of educational opportunities is not so great a loss as might be supposed, for many do not desire to have them. So far from making a fetish of school education, they doubt its value and think that their children are better employed in learning their father's trade or helping him in the fields. Many too are not without Brahmans to minister to them, though the latter are of a low type of hedge priests. And, notwithstanding their poverty, it is noticeable that many of them, especially those who have an admixture of aboriginal blood, seem to be much more cheerful and light-hearted than their somewhat sombre caste superiors.

Bad also as the condition of the untouchables still is, it is far better in many ways than it used to be. Before British rule was introduced they were looked on as Yahoos and treated in some parts as a race apart without the common rights of man. In Malabar and elsewhere in South India a Nair could kill an untouchable who did not take the trouble to get out of his way. James Forbes wrote: "If a Nair accidentally meets a Pooleah on the highway, he cuts him down with as little ceremony as we should destroy a noxious animal".[1] The same writer tells us that a Maratha proclamation issued at Baroch in 1783 ordered that no one of three untouchable castes (Halalkhor, Dheḍ, and Chandal) should upon any consideration come out of their houses after nine o'clock in the morning lest they should taint the air or touch the superior Hindus in the streets. Members of one section of the Koragas of South Canara were not even allowed to spit on the highway because of their utter impurity

1 *Oriental Memoirs* (1834), vol. 1, p. 254.

but had to spit into pots suspended from their necks; their name of Ande, or pot, Koragas commemorates their ancient shame.[1]

In Travancore some of the untouchable castes were literally slaves or serfs, and were given away, bought, sold and mortgaged like other property. It was not till 1855 that that State issued a proclamation liberating all State slaves, forbidding the law courts to admit the claim of any slave owner, and allowing slaves the right to hold property and to obtain redress for injuries. In this State the untouchables were subject to many vexatious restrictions, such as being forbidden to wear shoes or carry umbrellas; but what was most felt and resented was a State order that Shanan women should not wear any clothing above the waist. This order was withdrawn in deference to representations made by the British Government, though at first in a somewhat grudging manner. In 1859 a proclamation was issued that there was "no objection to Shanan women either putting on a jacket, like the Christian Shanan women, or to Shanan women of all creeds dressing in coarse cloth and tying themselves round with it, as the Mukkavattigals do,[2] or to their covering their bosoms

[1] E. Thurston, *Castes and Tribes of Southern India* (1909), vol. III, p. 428.

[2] A low fishing caste. This meant tying the cloth horizontally across the breasts, leaving the shoulders bare.

in any manner whatever, but not like women of high castes".[1] The objection to untouchable men wearing coats still lingers in backward areas in southern India, so much so that one who ventures to wear one may be beaten by men of higher caste.

The untouchables have representatives in the legislatures in British India, and an equal right to enter Government service, attend public educational institutions, etc. Equality in regard to Government service is, however, mainly an equality of opportunity, of which they are seldom in a position to take advantage because they are, generally speaking, the poorest and least educated section of the population. They are also debarred from the enjoyment of other rights by the opposition and sometimes the actual persecution of their co-religionists: the customs of a people cannot be quickly changed by official mandates. Hindu judges in outlying places have been known to be influenced by prejudice. According to evidence given in Madras before the Lee Commission in 1924, untouchables in such places and before such judges were not permitted to enter the courts, even though they were parties to a case or witnesses, but had to stand afar off, and their examination was con-

[1] See S. Mateer, *The Land of Charity. A Descriptive Account of Travancore and its People* (1870), pp. 41, 43, 44, 61, 305, 306.

ducted by a go-between who would go out, question them, and take back their answers to the judge.[1] In the State of Jaipur there were, as late as 1911, separate courts of law for untouchables; in the streets they had to give warning of their presence by calling out *Payse* or *Parayse* (Keep at a distance); and a sweeper was required to wear a crow's feather on his turban to show his unclean caste. Here, too, low castes, though admitted to the ordinary courts, could not hand in papers direct to the judge, but had them conveyed to him through other hands.[2]

The British Government has insisted on the untouchables having a right of admission to, and equal treatment in, publicly managed schools, besides stimulating a demand for education among them by means of special scholarships and remission of fees. But its efforts are often stultified by the opposition of higher castes. Schools maintained from public funds are open to all and no one can be refused admission because of his caste; but if untouchables take advantage of these facilities, one of three things is apt to happen. Their children may be allowed to attend school on sufferance, provided they sit apart from other children; or their life, or that of

[1] See Sir Reginald Craddock, *The Dilemma in India* (1929), p. 24.

[2] *Census Report of Rajputana and Ajmer-Merwara for 1911*, Part I, p. 264.

their parents, may be made miserable till they are withdrawn; or the school may be boycotted altogether. In 1931 an untouchable woman in Baroda was brutally assaulted and her crop destroyed because she had sent her son to a public elementary school. This was by no means an extraordinary case. A Committee which was appointed to consider the question of extending education in Saidapet, a suburb of Madras city, reported in the same year that Hindus of higher grades used every refinement of social and economic boycott to compel untouchables to withdraw their children from the public schools, even to the extent of combining to deny their families employment, food and shelter. The untouchables themselves preferred separate schools—not unnaturally under the circumstances—and the Committee was forced to the conclusion that the best thing was not to struggle against caste prejudice. Accordingly it recommended that the policy of Government requiring public schools to admit untouchables should be modified and separate schools opened for them so as to save them from persecution and prevent communal friction. Special schools of this class have been opened, and in the opinion of many this is the most hopeful line of advance.

The question of water supply creates a similar problem. There is no difficulty in cities or towns which have a public water supply of a modern type, with water laid on in pipes and drawn from hydrants and taps. The position is different in villages where the people obtain their water either from rivers or from tanks or from wells dug by themselves or their landlords. Where there is a flowing river, the untouchables can draw water from it at a point lower down the stream, and this is no great hardship. There is also no friction if they have separate wells or tanks. But where there are common tanks and wells, they are often denied access to them. If public funds have been used for a public tank or well, local authorities may direct that all should share in the water, but it is most difficult to enforce an order of this kind, for once the well or tank is in use, the villagers are in command of the situation. One example of their intolerance will suffice. In a village in Baroda an artesian well was sunk in 1931 with labour supplied by untouchables on the understanding that they would have a right to use it. When it was ready, they were refused access to it, but eventually were allowed to lay a separate pipe 500 feet long with a tap at the end for their exclusive use. This having been done, the castes living at the end of the pipe objected, and the untouchables were left as badly off for water as before.

On the other hand, the untouchables themselves have caste prejudices just as much as their superiors. In some parts they too will refuse to draw water from the same well, and different untouchable castes must have different wells. A recent report of the State Well-Sinking Department of Hyderabad states that, except for objecting to wells for outcastes being sunk close to their own, the higher castes gave little trouble. Far more trouble was caused by the caste prejudices of the untouchables. In one case some liberal-minded Brahmans even drank water pumped by men of low untouchable castes, as an object lesson. This was wasted on the untouchables of higher rank, who were irreconcilable, declaring that they would never take water from a pump on which a man of a lower rank laid a finger.

There has been for some years past a strong movement among the untouchables aiming at the improvement of their status and the removal of their social and religious disabilities. A large number no longer acquiesce in their subjection, but have acquired a new outlook, owing to such causes as greater wealth and the spread of education. Their feeling is like that of the negro slave saying "Am I not a man and a brother?" They have begun to organize and assert themselves, and their efforts have the sympathy of many progressive Hindus of the higher castes. The Legislative Council in Madras passed in 1930–1 an Act affirming the right of all classes and communities, irrespective of caste and creed, to have access to, and make use of, all public places, such as streets, markets and tanks maintained from municipal funds, and rendering an obstruction to their use an offence punishable by fine. The Bombay Legislative Council and many local bodies have also passed resolutions affirming their equal rights to benefit from public institutions (schools, sources of water-supply, etc.); but this is only too often done as a gesture and without any real effort to implement the resolutions.

Orthodox Brahmans oppose the pretensions of the untouchables with might and main: at present attempts to assert and enforce a right to admission to temples in Bombay is meeting with equally determined opposition. In Madras the antagonism between them and higher castes has led to outbreaks of fierce fanaticism. The history of the struggle of the Shanans to better themselves is one of particular turbulence. As far back as 1858 there were riots in Travancore because women converts to Christianity took to wearing clothes above the waist. In 1899 their claim to enter temples in Tinnevelly and the opposition offered by other castes produced serious riots, accompanied by arson and pillage on both sides, in which thousands were engaged. The outbreaks were so grave and widespread that a military force had to be drafted to the district to suppress them.

Again, in 1902 rioting broke out in the same district in consequence of a decision of the Shanans that their women should not carry loads on their heads nor go to market and that they should be free to wear better ornaments than leaden bracelets and beads.

Sometimes the untouchables, acting on Mr Gandhi's teaching of non-violence, seek to attain their aims by passive means. They show a dogged persistence which is met with equal doggedness on the part of the Brahmans, as may be seen from a prolonged but peaceful struggle which took place some years ago at Vaikam in the State of Travancore. There, a famous temple stands at the junction of four roads, and the untouchables were not allowed to come along any of them within a certain distance of the shrine. They began to demand a right of way, and the State authorities, wishing to maintain the *status quo*, set up barriers across the roads. These were guarded by police, and only those who were free from the taint of untouchability were allowed through. Every day some untouchables presented themselves at the barriers and, when they were stopped, sat down in front of them and remained there the livelong day with nothing to break the monotony of their watch but spinning on the spinning wheel. This quiet but ineffective siege went on for over a year, a few Brahman sympathizers joining the parties outside the barriers, sharing their watch and their meals, and of course losing their caste. At last Mr Gandhi visited the town and on his intercession the barriers were removed and the roads thrown open to all.[1]

Many of the untouchables themselves are reluctant to join in such movements, largely because of ignorance and religious sentiment, which makes them believe that their low position is not merely natural but divinely instituted. Mr J. T. Gwynne found this sentiment strongly at work even in Bardoli in Gujarat, a stronghold of Mr Gandhi, who has denounced untouchability as an intolerable system which has degraded Indian humanity. The untouchables there, Mr Gwynne wrote in 1922,

> had heard that Mahatma Gandhi was telling the caste ryot[2] that he should touch them and admit them into the schools. But they did not desire this. It would be a sin for them to touch a caste man. This confirms what non-co-operating ryots have told me, that, having with difficulty overcome their own scruples about touching an "untouchable", they found still greater difficulty in surmounting the "untouchable's" scruples about being touched.[3]

"The helpless condition of the depressed

[1] See W. E. S. Holland, *The Indian Outlook* (1926), pp. 76–80.

[2] The cultivator.

[3] *Indian Politics* (1924), p. 72.

classes must be attributed entirely to the dogged and the determined opposition of the whole mass of the orthodox population." This is the view expressed by two delegates to the Round Table Conference, Dr B. R. Ambedkar and Rao Bahadur Srinivasan (President of the Madras Depressed Classes Federation), in a statement setting forth the position and political claims of the depressed classes. The attitude of their fellow Hindus towards them has, however, changed considerably owing to two influences, one philanthropic, the other political. A humanitarian movement for their uplift has been inaugurated and maintained by liberal-minded and advanced Hindus. The Servants of India Society, founded by the late Mr G. K. Gokhale with the object of working for the good of India by social service and other means, irrespective of caste and creed, has done good pioneer work. Several other societies have been started for their educational and social benefit: in Bengal one was founded by Lord Sinha of Raipur; in Baroda the Maharaja Gaekwar founded the Depressed Classes Institute. Unfortunately philanthropic work is apt to be thwarted by the obstructiveness of less educated Hindu reactionaries. In 1929 a Brahman in the United Provinces was brutally murdered by eight other Brahmans because he had recognized the untouchables of his village as men and brothers, taken water brought by them, and helped them with bricks when, on his advice, they set about building a temple of their own.

The angle of vision of the upper classes has changed much of late years owing to political influences. A generation ago orthodox Hindus regarded the untouchables as outside the pale of Hinduism and did not scruple to say so. A Bengali Brahman, Mr U. N. Mukharji, merely reflected current opinion when he wrote in 1909:

> It is all one to the Brahmans whether they call themselves Hindus or not. They are just as much untouchables as they were before. Their adoption of the Hindu religion causes some amount of amusement and sometimes gives rise to a certain amount of indulgent contempt.

A Hari or Dom (both untouchables) and a dog would, he declared, be hunted out of a place of worship with equally little ceremony and with equally little hesitation. "If anything the dog will get off more cheaply than the other two, as they are supposed to know better."[1] Few now would be so outspoken, at any rate in public. The same views may be held, but it is not thought politic to express them. A change has come over the scene since the introduction of the Montagu-Chelmsford political reforms and the separate representation of Moslems. Communal passions

[1] See *A Dying Race* (Calcutta, 1909), pp. 34, 37–8.

have risen high and Hindu politicians have realized that the untouchables are not a negligible quantity. There has been real anxiety that they should not be driven into the fold of either Islam or Christianity and so decrease the numerical strength and voting power of Hindus;[1] and in some provinces they are beginning to show that politically they are a force to be reckoned with.

Opinion still differs widely as to the social treatment they should receive. Some are in favour of improving their economic condition and keeping them down socially, others are ready to remove the social ban on them as well as to promote their material welfare. The old reactionary school still sets its face against any measures for their uplift. Mr Gandhi himself has taken up their cause and in 1931 declared in *Young India* that when Swaraj is established,

> there will be no untouchability. The untouchables will have the same rights as any other.... The Brahman will not be able, as some are now, to punish the untouchables

[1] These fears are not imaginary. In 1895 the Shanans in part of Tinevelly became Roman Catholics *en masse* because of the treatment they received. In 1931 it was reported from Nagpur that 100 stone-masons had embraced Islam in disgust at not being allowed to draw water from a public well and that 200 more threatened to follow their example. In South India, where the untouchable convert to Islam or Christianity is not thought to cause pollution by proximity like the Hindu untouchable, the inducement to forsake Hinduism is particularly great.

for daring to walk in the public streets or for using public wells. Under Swaraj there will be no such scandal as that of the use of public temples being denied to untouchables when allowed to other Hindus.

This, of course, is a question of the future and depends on the attainment of that indefinite ideal, Swaraj. It is a different thing to translate it into present practice; and it is significant that a few years ago, when Mr Gandhi urged the abolition of untouchability in the city of Bombay, he roused a storm of opposition among orthodox Hindus and was threatened with personal violence.

Chapter IX

MODERN TENDENCIES

DURING the present century the caste system has been subject to many disintegrating influences. Reformers have attacked it both on political and social grounds. It has been denounced on the one hand as an obstacle to the growth of nationalism, and on the other as a denial of the inherent rights of every man to liberty and the pursuit of happiness. A new spirit of service has sprung up among the younger men of the educated classes; and some of the more ardent spirits have not hesitated to do things which formerly would have been regarded with horror, such as nursing untouchables during epidemics of plague and malaria and even carrying out and burning their dead bodies.

The domination of the Brahman has also been challenged by the non-Brahman in some parts. In Bombay the Lingayats have never acknowledged the Brahmans as their priests, and, according to Mr Crooke, there is no part of India in which Brahmans are held in less estimation in spite of the fact that they acted as Mayors of the Palace to the Maratha rulers.[1] In this province

[1] *Things Indian* (1906), p. 65.

an association called the *Satya Shodak Samāj*, i.e. the Society of Truth and Purity, was founded as long ago as 1873 with the object of delivering non-Brahmans from subjection to Brahmans not only in social but also in religious matters. Non-Brahmans were to be instructed in religious rites and ceremonies in order that they might be independent of the Brahmans. The services of the latter were to be dispensed with, and the non-Brahmans themselves were to officiate instead. The basic principle of the movement was that there was no need for any intermediary between the gods and men. It made a direct attack on the authority of the Brahmans and on the belief that no ceremonies could be efficacious unless performed by them. The Society languished for a time but has shown renewed vigour during the present century. Primarily a religious and social movement, it has assumed a political character, and seeks to secure for non-Brahmans not only the improvement of their social condition but also a share of political power and to prevent the Brahmans having any monopoly of it. The non-Brahman movement in Bombay is at present strong only in the south of the presidency.[1]

There has been a stronger challenge to Brahman domination in the Madras presidency. The

[1] See *Indian Statutory Commission's Report* (1930), vol. VII, pp. 226–30.

non-Brahman movement there began by aiming at social reform but found politics more absorbing and also likely to give quicker results. The immediate result of the elections held in 1920 under the Montagu-Chelmsford Reforms scheme was a victory for the non-Brahman party, which had been formed with the object of ending the political predominance of the Brahmans. It was called the Justice party, as it aimed at doing justice to all sections of the community irrespective of caste or creed. Its motto was "Equal opportunities for all and injustice to none". A non-Brahman Ministry was formed, which promptly proceeded to ensure favourable treatment for non-Brahmans in the matter of appointments to the public services and local bodies, besides pursuing a liberal policy in regard to education, public health and local self-government: a Public Service Commission now allocates appointments in Madras with a fixed ratio to caste. The formation of a party on caste lines as the immediate result of the introduction of the representative system is a remarkable sign of the vital importance of caste in national life.

The Justice party, which is a strong force in Madras, forms the political side of a movement of which the social side is represented by what is called the "self-respect movement", which is concerned with social reform. In both its aspects the movement is opposed to the working of the caste system. Describing its aims, Rao Bahadur Sir A. P. Patro, a former Minister of the Madras Government and the present leader of the Justice party, says:

The Justice movement is organized for the vindication of self-respect. Social justice is the basic principle of its foundation. At one time the Shastras were looked up to as giving authority for caste domination, but the progress of events altered men's minds, and the movement demands in the interests of national progress the abandonment of caste bigotry and intellectual arrogance. There was a time when authority took the place of reason and judgement, when all matters social and religious were controlled by the powerful hierarchy of priesthood, to whom alone higher education in the Shastras and general culture were restricted. This has to give way and is slowly making room for individual freedom and individual culture. Our ideas on many social customs have undergone radical changes; we have begun to discourage, if not to discard, caste and priestly authority.[1]

In addition to movements from within, the caste system has been affected by other influences, largely of European origin, of which the changes in industrial conditions may first be mentioned. India, that land of contrasts, is a land of villages but is also one of the eight principal industrial countries of the world. Its

[1] *The Justice Movement in India*, *Asiatic Review*, January, 1932, p. 28.

great manufactures and industries are, in the main, concentrated in a few areas, and in those areas they have had a strong influence in relaxing the bonds of caste. Men of different castes have to work together in the mills, factories and mines under conditions which are incompatible with the strict observance of caste customs. Outside them the adjuncts of modern civilization, railway trains, trams and motor omnibuses have had a similar effect. Railway and other transport companies are not respecters of caste, and all who take tickets have an equal right to travel, though a case has been known of untouchables being forced by their fellow-passengers to ride on the top of a motor-bus.

Nothing, however, has done so much to weaken the observance of caste customs as the spread of education and the impact of western ideas. This is chiefly noticeable among the higher castes, whose members have had the greatest share of higher education. The old ideas about food and drink, occupations and ceremonial observances, have to a large extent given way before considerations of material interest and convenience. The reaction against caste restrictions has been going on a long time. Sir Surendranath Banerjea, a Kulin Brahman of Bengal, has shown that even sixty years ago a Bengali Brahman could do much as he liked in the matter of food.

"My father", he wrote, "was by no means orthodox in his ways and his transgressions against strict orthodoxy were numerous and grave; but a visit to England was not one of them. Forbidden food and drink he used to take with an ostentation that shocked my grandfather. But Hindu society said nothing, winked at it, forgot and forgave."

The old prejudice against sea voyages, however, was still strong. When Sir Surendranath Banerjea returned from England in 1871, his family was practically outcasted for such a glaring offence against orthodoxy.

"In the meantime", he added, "a silent and stupendous change has taken place. A sea voyage or a visit to Europe no longer involves the loss of caste. Among the Brahmans, especially in the Mofussil,[1] there may be some squeamishness; but among other castes a man may visit any part of the world he pleases, and yet retain his social status as a member of the caste....Fifty years ago, I was an outcaste (being an England-returned Brahman) in the village where I live. To-day I am an honoured member of the community."[2]

Even in regard to marriage some advanced sections of the higher castes, such as Brahmans and Kayasths in Bengal, have reformed sufficiently to permit intermarriages between subcastes; and as the Brahmans set the standard, some low castes have followed suit. There have

[1] Rural areas.
[2] *A Nation in Making* (1925), pp. 25, 26, 398.

also been isolated cases of widow remarriage. A great sensation was caused in Calcutta some years ago by Sir Ashutosh Mukharji, a Brahman of avowed orthodoxy, who was a Judge of the High Court, allowing his daughter to contract a second marriage; but such cases are still rare.[1]

The old order is also waning among the high castes in Madras, except in matters relating to marriage.

"There are few things", wrote Mr J. Chartres Molony, "that the high-caste Indian may not do and retain his caste, so long as he remains loyal to the strange (at least in European opinion) system of exclusiveness devised to keep the outer world from entering within the pale of his community. The "casteman" of modern days exchanges his *dhoti* and *angavastram* for coat and trousers, crops his luxuriant top-knot, dilutes his soda, preserves a discreet incuriosity as to the nature of his food and its cooking, modestly refrains from dinning the ears of Heaven with a superfluity of prayers, and the withers of orthodox society remain unwrung. But he must not as yet trample down the sacred fence by a marriage outside his particular fold, or create a possibility of such trampling, by postponing the marriage of his daughter to an age when natural feelings might clash rudely with abstract principles."[2]

The infection of modern ideas seems equally strong among the high castes in Bombay.

1 The marriage of Hindu widows was legalized by an Act passed in 1856.

2 *Madras Census Report for 1911*, Part I, p. 178.

Little or no notice is taken of a catholic taste for food. Marriages of the orthodox with Europeanized free-thinkers who eat meat and drink liquor are permitted, and caste is quietly resumed by those who have returned from Europe, though practice in this respect is not altogether uniform: the Gaud Sarasvats of Bombay are divided into two sections called the "Londoners" and the "non-Londoners", of which the former consists of those who were excommunicated for dining with persons who had returned from Europe, and the latter of those who retained their caste honour. The laxity of some high castes has become proverbial: according to a popular proverb, "A Kanbi is never an outcaste and a Garasia never polluted".[1]

It would also appear from the account given by Dr Ketkar that the Chitpavan Brahman outside orthodox circles has become almost a law unto himself.

> A man who belongs to the caste which represents priesthood may commit any infraction of the rules of convention or of scripture, or may do actions which even many non-priestly castes prohibit. He may even engage in any trade he pleases. He may go and eat where he wants to, drink anything he desires, and act according to the manners of the foreign country, may refuse to make atonement for what a traditionalist Hindu regards as sin, and may still retain his position in the community,

[1] *Bombay Census Report for 1911*, Part 1, p. 255.

that is, may claim membership of the sacred priestly caste, and his claim would go unchallenged. Even after doing all this, if he cares to take up the occupation of a priest, nobody would be able to prevent him from doing so. Such is the latitude which men who belong to the Chittapavan Brahman caste can take.[1]

The same writer is eloquent on the subject of the weakening of the control exercised by Brahmans over the higher castes. In Poona Sastris and Pandits frequently excommunicate men who have been to England or have married widows or drunk tea with Englishmen, but no one takes any notice of their fiats outside their own circle, which has become very small and unimportant. "The excommunication by the assemblies of priests and Pandits has become a joke."[2]

A clear line of distinction should be drawn between conditions in the cities and conditions in the villages, which, it must not be forgotten, contain nine-tenths of the population. The village community, it has been well said, has always been and still is the social cell in India. To the ordinary Hindu the village is his world, and village opinion is most conservative. In social matters it is in a large measure moulded by the women, who cling to the old ways. Their outlook is circumscribed by convention and custom, and they cherish the family honour,

[1] S. V. Ketkar, *An Essay on Hinduism* (1911), p. 87.
[2] *Ibid.* p. 83.

which depends on adherence to caste custom. In particular, the grandmother, whose influence is especially great, stands for the maintenance of orthodox tradition, ceremony, and propriety: referring to her power and her conservatism, Lord Curzon is said to have made the shrewd remark that what India needs is a new grandmother. Women are becoming to a certain extent emancipated in the cities: nothing has done so much in this direction as the political fervour of the civil disobedience movement, which has brought women out of *purdah* in an extraordinary way; but in the villages they remain so conservative as to be actually reactionary.

It is the absence of home influences which accounts in a large measure for men throwing off restraints in the cities. It is customary for men to go and work in them for a time, leaving their families at home: in Calcutta there are more than twice as many men as women, and in Bombay the preponderance of males is even greater. Their permanent homes are mostly in the villages, and when they return there, the old influences resume their sway. The people themselves recognize and deplore the laxity of town life: in Madras there is a proverb to the effect that a quarter of the usual caste observances suffices in the towns.

A distinction must also be drawn between the more highly educated higher castes and the less educated lower castes. Laxity which is winked at among the former is punished among the latter, perhaps because they feel that if they sacrifice pride of caste, they sacrifice everything. So far from wishing for the abolition of caste because of the low estate to which it condemns them, they cling to the system in the hope of rising to higher place. Even the untouchables, whose awakening in recent years has been so remarkable a phenomenon, merely wish to be free from their present disabilities and to attain to a higher rank in the same social system. Envy, and not resentment, is the general feeling of the lower towards the higher castes. They do not want so much to put down the mighty from their seats as to put themselves in the seats of the mighty. Hence the upward surge of the lower castes; hence their tendency to assume the sacred thread as if they had a right to it and to claim recognition as one of the traditional twice-born *varnas*: one caste, the Goalas of Bihar, were so little consistent that one year they claimed to be Vaisyas and another they wanted to climb higher and rank as Kshattriyas. Although, however, the lower castes struggle to ascend the social ladder, they are individually insistent that those below them should not rise higher.

The vitality of caste is very much in evidence at each decennial census. There is a general idea that the object of a census is not merely to enumerate the number of persons belonging to different castes, but also to fix their relative precedence. Each census is the occasion for considerable excitement and active agitation on the subject. The census officers are embarrassed by the numerous and often fantastic claims put forward. Hundreds of petitions and memorials are received demanding that the different castes shall be recorded under new-fangled honorific names, or shall be recognized as Brahmans, Kshattriyas and Vaisyas, or shall be given a higher rank in an imaginary warrant of precedence. When I was in charge of the census of Bengal in 1911, the mere weight of the paper used for the memorials sent to me was over a hundredweight. Nor is agitation confined to writing. Some of the lower castes are truculent and threaten violence if they are not recorded under some other names. In 1921 the Jugis, a low weaver caste in Bengal, who claimed to be Brahmans, wanted to be returned as Jogis by caste and to have the names of their women written down in the schedules as Devi, a name used by Brahman women. One district officer received notice of a civil suit because a Jugi woman's name had been recorded as Dasi and not as Devi. On the other hand, a Brahman enumerator declared that he would rather cut off his hand than write down the name of these low caste women as Devi. So much bitterness and ill-feeling are aroused that meetings have been held urging the omission of caste returns from the census on the ground that they perpetuate the subjection of the low castes and hinder progress towards social equality. As a matter of fact, the census sometimes helps the low castes by giving official recognition to new names free from the humiliating associations of the old names. In this way the Chandals of Bengal got rid of their old name with its immemorial tradition of shame, and are known by the more pleasing designation of Namasudra.

Apart from temporary ebullitions at the time of the census the lower castes are steadily endeavouring to enhance their social prestige by abandoning their own customs and adopting those of the higher castes. So far is this leaven at work that it is becoming increasingly difficult to obtain information about peculiar traditional customs, often of great interest to the anthropologist, because they are ashamed of them and will even deny knowledge of them. The results of their ambition are not always healthy, for a low caste which desires to ape the manners of Brahmans and other high castes tends to give up the practice of widow remarriage and to introduce that of child marriage (as regards the ceremony and not the consummation of marriage): the prohibition of widow remarriage in particular is regarded as a *cachet* of respectability.

Other measures by which an improvement of status is sought are the abandonment of occupations thought to be degrading, the adoption of vegetarianism instead of meat-eating, and a self-denying ordinance against the drinking of liquor.

Another modern development is the formation of caste associations, called *Sabhās* in northern India (or *Samitis* in Bengal), which hold annual conferences and are organized like European associations or societies. One Bengal caste, which is mainly engaged in a form of market-gardening, actually formed a company with shareholders and directors. The Ahirs or Goalas, whose association includes members from all over northern India, publishes a monthly journal. The object is in all cases the same, viz. the improvement of the position of the caste; in all cases the spread of education is put in the forefront of the programme together with measures of social reform. Modern influences are apparent in the conception of the latter, for, instead of imitating high castes by introducing earlier marriages, many are now in favour of postponing the age of marriage. One of the lowest of the castes of Bengal, the Namasudras, resolved at a general conference in 1908 that any man who married a son under the age of twenty or a daughter under ten should be excommunicated. The Dosadhs of Bihar, another low caste, came to an agreement that the ages should be fifteen and ten years respectively; the Goalas in the same area also pronounced against child marriage; the Mehtars, who are Moslems by religion and scavengers by profession, not to be outdone, resolved that no child under three years of age should be given in marriage. Associations of this kind supplement, and do not replace, the caste councils, to which the internal government of the castes is left. They are concerned not with the cases of individuals, but with lines of policy, and their general effect is to maintain caste solidarity.

On a survey of the whole situation it may be said that though there is a certain neglect of some canons of conduct, the lines of cleavage between different castes have been neither obliterated nor obscured. There is a tendency, more especially among the educated sections of the upper classes, to abandon or modify caste customs, but there is no general revolt against the system. Forms may be changed, but fundamentally caste remains the same. Those who would sweep away abuses would leave the main edifice intact. Even untouchables, in all their anxiety to remove the stigma of birth, rarely suggest the total abolition of caste. The rebellion of these and other low castes against the place assigned to them in the system rests on the assumption that that system will remain. Hindu reformers who condemn untouchability also maintain that a caste system, though not perhaps in its present form, is essential to Hinduism. It is its association with religion which gives caste so much of its vitality and strength: it is a social system sanctified by religion. Conversely, the caste system helps to preserve Hinduism which, as observed by Max Müller, rests on the system of caste as on a rock which no arguments can shake: one of the objections made by educated Hindus to Christianity is that it has a levelling tendency, which is against all the traditions and principles of the caste system.

The tendency of even advanced thinkers to maintain the caste system, while discarding some of the features which disfigure it, is exemplified by Mr Gandhi's attitude towards it. He has declared that he is satisfied that caste is a healthy institution, but regards untouchability, which sanctions "the Satanic treatment of our kith and kin", as the greatest blot on Hinduism. He derides irrational regulations about food and drink, by which, in his opinion, Hinduism is resolving itself into a set of elaborate rules as to what and with whom to eat; and he remarks: "India is a country of nonsense. It is nonsensical to parch one's throat with thirst when a kindly Muhammadan is ready to offer pure water to drink, and yet thousands of Hindus would rather die of thirst than drink water from a Muhammadan household".

At the same time Mr Gandhi holds that *varna*, by which he means caste in a Vedic sense, is the law of heredity, the predetermination of a man's profession. The law of *varna*, he asserts, is that a man shall follow the profession of his ancestors for the purpose of earning his living, and this he calls an immutable law of nature. Religious duty includes the environment in which we were placed at birth by God. It connotes living in harmony with those birth conditions and not rebelling against them or seeking to overpass their limitations. The *varna* determines a man's calling but does not restrict or regulate social intercourse. Accordingly neglect of the prohibition on interdining or even intermarriage does not necessarily deprive a man of the caste status which birth has given, but this prohibition is necessary for a rapid evolution of the soul, and Mr Gandhi would not personally agree to a marriage out of caste.[1]

The religious associations of caste are not without their drawbacks. On account of them irrational practices which have no real religious basis are thought to be part and parcel of Hinduism; the accretions of custom are treated as if they were fundamental principles; and proof of the absence of scriptural sanction does not shake popular belief in their necessity: there

[1] C. F. Andrews, *Mahatma Gandhi's Ideas* (1929), pp. 35, 36, 38, 128, 129, 176, 354.

is a saying of a Hindu sage that custom decides everything and overrides scriptural law. Lord William Bentinck wisely observed, when the prohibition of suttee was under discussion, that it was an evasion of the real difficulties to try to prove that it was not essentially a part of the Hindu religion, and pertinently pointed out that the question was not what the rite was but what it was supposed to be. The attitude of the masses in such matters is like that of a learned Brahman mentioned by Colonel Sleeman in *Rambles and Recollections of an Indian Official*. During the rule of the Marathas human sacrifices used to be offered in the cities of Sagar (Saugor) until they were put an end to in 1800 by a Maratha Governor. A Brahman told Sleeman that his humane order had led to the ruin of the Governor's family and government, and remarked: "There is no sin in not offering human sacrifices to the gods when none have been offered; but where the gods have been accustomed to them, they are very naturally annoyed when the rite is abolished and visit the place and people with all kinds of calamity". Sleeman himself added that perhaps three Brahman priests out of four would have argued in the same manner.

For the majority of Hindus, caste is the sphere within which morality operates. That morality may in some respects seem strange to European thoughts, but there is no question of the real value of caste in inculcating and maintaining principles of self-restraint. It is chiefly caste which checks vice and keeps up the standard of propriety, particularly among the lower castes. Take away the caste honour of the low caste man, and you destroy the basis of his virtues. As pointed out by the Abbé Dubois, in *Hindu Manners and Customs*, the shame which would reflect on a whole caste if the faults of one of its individual members went unpunished guarantees that the caste will execute justice, defend its own honour, and keep all its members within the bounds of duty.

This aspect of the question should not be overlooked in the common chorus of condemnation of the evils of caste. The latter are patent. Caste is hide-bound and fettered by inhibitions which may have been reasonable in inception but have become unreasonable. It sets up artificial standards of value and it is hostile to reform. It circumscribes the sphere both of sympathy and of co-operation. It limits individual initiative and it is an obstacle to national unity and progress. A Hindu is primarily a member of a caste and not of a nation; his loyalty is to a group and not to the general community. There can be no united national life so long as society is split up into thousands of separate sections, each guided by its own canons of conduct and not by a common public opinion.

There can be little social progress so long as men of low caste, however educated they may be, whatever position they may have attained in Government service, in commerce, or in the professions, are condemned by the stigma of birth to lifelong social inferiority or even degradation.

On the other hand, caste, like other human institutions, has its good points, which ought to be recognized. It forms a bond of social and religious union among its members and stimulates a corporate spirit which would otherwise often be lacking. It acts in a certain degree as a charitable institution, and, where there is a common occupation, it has some of the characteristics of a trade union. But it does its best work as a guardian of morality. It is caste which habituates Hindus to that respect for authority and exercise of self-restraint which form the basis of social order. In the past it has helped to save Hindu society from disintegration and Hindu culture from destruction. Through successive conquests and revolutions it has been a stable force, and its stabilizing influence is not without political importance at the present time, when the communist movement is said to be a menace to India.[1] A system which is permeated by religion is utterly opposed to the Bolshevist doctrine of a war upon religion. The idea of a class war is alien to a people which believes that

[1] *India in 1929–30* (Calcutta, 1931), p. 10.

the social hierarchy is divinely ordained and that equality is not only contrary to experience but is impossible because each man's state of life is predetermined by his actions in past lives.

Many thoughtful Indians are therefore strongly in favour of the caste system on the ground that it is a bulwark of society against revolutionary assaults. On the other hand, its abolition is urged by others as a necessary condition of popular government. The views of this school of thought have recently been expressed by Rao Bahadur Sir A. P. Patro, who has pointed out that power cannot safely be vested in the people unless the mental habit which sanctions and enforces the customary treatment of lower castes and races is changed—the habit of mind which he calls "slave mentality and unreasoning submission to priestly class or politician".

"Everything", he writes, "that awakens the Indian ryot's[1] intelligence and which helps him to be an independent, self-relying man, everything that breaks the barriers of caste and community and prepares a mentality to regard one another as neighbours, will truly and effectively hasten the day when the goal of full responsible government will be reached. The dream of Indian nationalism will be realized fully with the passing away of caste from our land."[2]

[1] The cultivator.

[2] *The Justice Movement in India*, *Asiatic Review*, January 1932, pp. 28, 31, 33.

The abolition of the caste system seems, however, an ideal which is not likely to be realized except in the dim and distant future; and to those who hope for the weakening of its hold upon the people it is disappointing to find that candidates for election to the legislature of one province solicit the votes of their castemen simply on the strength of caste fellowship without regard to other considerations, that a solid caste vote has determined the result of some elections, and that there has been a tendency in the legislature itself for groups to be formed on caste lines.[1]

[1] B. Abdy Collins, *Bihar and Orissa in 1925–26* (Patna, 1927), p. 4.

Index